The Second Book of the
GREAT MUSICIANS

Books by
Percy A. Scholes

The Listener's Guide to Music
The First Book of the Great Musicians
The Second Book of the Great Musicians
The Third Book of the Great Musicians
The Complete Book of the Great Musicians

The Second Book of the
GREAT MUSICIANS

*A Further Course in Appreciation
for Young Readers*

by

Percy A. Scholes

YESTERDAY'S CLASSICS

ITHACA, NEW YORK

This edition, first published in 2021 by Yesterday's Classics, an imprint of Yesterday's Classics, LLC, is an unabridged republication of the text originally published by Oxford Univeristy Press in 1922. For the complete listing of the books that are published by Yesterday's Classics, please visit www.yesterdaysclassics. com. Yesterday's Classics is the publishing arm of Gateway to the Classics which presents the complete text of hundreds of classic books for children at www. gatewaytotheclassics.com.

ISBN: 978-1-63334-129-6

Yesterday's Classics, LLC
PO Box 339
Ithaca, NY 14851

TO THE READER

HERE is a Second Book of the Great Musicians—for those who have already read the first one. As whilst they have been reading it they have been growing older and cleverer, I have not used such simple language this time as I did before, and I have made the chapters rather longer and fuller. I want to offer a word of thanks to Mr. Emery Walker, as well as to Mr. F. Page of the Oxford University Press, who have taken a great deal of trouble to help me to find suitable pictures to illustrate this book, and to Mr. W. R. Anderson, Editor of the monthly journal, *The Music Teacher*, who has read the proofs for me. A Third Book of the Great Musicians is in preparation and will complete the series.

The Author

CONTENTS

I. SCHUBERT 1

II. THE INVENTOR OF THE
NOCTURNE: JOHN FIELD 15

III. MENDELSSOHN 27

IV. ABOUT THE OLD MIRACLE PLAYS
AND MASQUES, AND WHAT
SPRANG FROM THEM 39

V. ABOUT ORATORIOS 49

VI. THE EARLIEST OPERAS 57

VII. MORE ABOUT OPERA 65

VIII. WAGNER 76

IX. VERDI 89

X. THE GAME OF 'CAMOUFLAGED
TUNES' 98

XI. ORGANS 101

XII. DEBUSSY 114

XIII. MILITARY MUSIC 126

XIV. ARMY BANDS OF TODAY 131

XV. SULLIVAN 141

SCHUBERT

CHAPTER I

SCHUBERT

1797-1828

A School Band Practice

THE school orchestra was practising. The oboe and flute and bassoon and horn and kettle-drum were vigorously playing their parts or counting their rests, and the string players were fiddling away. One of the big boys was the leading Violin. It was a musical school, and this boy had been there a long time and could play beautifully. What were they playing? Well, for a guess, one of Haydn's symphonies. This school was in Vienna, and Haydn and Beethoven both lived in Vienna at that very time, and their music was popular with the Viennese; so we will suppose that the band was playing a Haydn symphony, since a Beethoven symphony is, as a rule, too difficult for a school orchestra. By and by came a break in the playing, as one movement of the symphony ended and before the next began, and the big boy, the leader (Spaun was his name), turned round to see who it could be who was playing behind him, with such firm rhythm and in such good tune.

There he saw a little new boy, a round-faced, curly-headed fellow, with spectacles. His name was Franz Schubert, but already he had a nickname—'The Miller', because when he came to be examined for entrance to the school he wore a light coat. Spaun nodded at him with approval, and then the playing began again. But when the practice was over he learnt more about 'The Miller', and in a few days he had become one of his truest friends.

School Joys and Troubles

Franz needed friends. His father was poor, and the school life, though happy in many ways, was in others a hard one. At the time Franz was admitted to this school he had ten or eleven brothers and sisters, and as years went by more came into the world, so that in the end there were seventeen children in the family. Now the father, though a hard-working man, did not earn a great deal of money. So when, to his great joy, he managed to get his clever son Franz into the school I have been speaking of, which was the Emperor's choir school, and trained the boys for the court chapel, he could not supply him with those little luxuries that boys at a boarding-school seem to expect, and it is quite certain, for instance, that Franz had no 'tuck box'. 'Tuck box' indeed! Why, he had not even enough plain wholesome food, as you may find from a letter he wrote some time after this to his elder brother, Ferdinand, who was his favourite brother and always, through his whole life, very good to him. This is what he wrote:

My dear Brother,

I have been thinking over my life here, and I find it's really not a bad one, on the whole, but there are some ways in which it could be improved. You know how much one enjoys a roll or an apple now and again, and all the more when one has to wait eight-and-a-half hours between dinner and supper! All the money Father gave me, which wasn't much, has gone long ago, so what am I to do? This is what I've been thinking—Can't you let me have a shilling or two a month? . . . .

You see, in those days, neither schoolmasters nor Emperors had any idea of making schoolboys comfortable. They had a notion that if you gave them plenty to eat and well-warmed rooms to work in (the rooms at this school had no fires in winter) the boys would be 'spoiled'. All the same, if you or I were an Emperor we would treat our choir-boys better, wouldn't we? and risk 'spoiling' them!

The Young Composer

Besides food and warmth there was something else of which young Franz felt the lack. He was already a composer, and composition was as necessary to his life as games are to yours. And he couldn't get music-paper. Here was a chance for the big boy, Spaun, to help him, and help him he did, so that Franz just poured out music—songs and piano pieces, and string quartets, and church anthems, all of which his school friends were willing and eager to try over as fast as they were written. It was really a splendid school for Franz, in that way, at any rate; there was plenty of music going on. But one thing he missed badly, and really suffered from all his life—though they taught the boys to sing and play, and had a rehearsal of the orchestra every day, nobody ever taught them to compose. So Franz had just to pick up composition as best he could, which was a pity, for even a born composer needs teaching, just as a born cricketer is all the better for some good coaching.

Holidays

You see that Franz lived in music, when at school, and so he did, too, at home, for when there came a holiday time, and he hurried home, he got to work at once with his father and brothers, playing away at string quartets. Franz played the Viola on these occasions, his father the 'Cello, and two brothers the first and second Violins. This family string quartet became well-known in the neighbourhood, and by and by was enlarged to a little band, by taking in other players, so that Haydn's symphonies could be played (with a bit of special arrangement); then neighbours liked to drop in and hear the music, and the room at home became too small, and so another and larger one was taken, and after that a still larger, and then the little band of musicians was increased to a full orchestra. All this time Franz went on playing the Viola, and also composing. In his last year at school he composed a symphony for the school orchestra, and later he wrote some symphonies for the home orchestra too.

Earning a Living

When Franz left school there was the question of what to do with him. He was determined to be a composer, but to earn a living by composing was even more difficult in those days than in these. So he decided to be a schoolmaster. His father was the master of a parish school in Vienna, and Franz joined him and taught the lowest class. I think he hated the work, and what he really liked was to slam the school door at the end of the day and get home to his composing, or else to run off to see his old friends at the Choir School and join them in their music-making, or take them some new music he had just written. About this time he began to have a few lessons in composition. There was in Vienna a musician named Salieri, the Emperor's chief musician (or 'Capellmeister'). He had helped Beethoven, in his earlier days, by advice and lessons, and now he helped Schubert in the same way, for he saw that the youth was a genius and was well worth helping.

How Schubert Wrote and Performed a Mass

One great event about this time (he was now seventeen) was Schubert's composition of a Mass for one of the churches. He conducted it himself, his brother played the organ, a celebrated violinist, called Mayseder, came and led the violins, and the performance went off very well and made quite a stir. To commemorate the occasion his father, who was delighted to see his son doing such great things, spent a good deal of his hardly-earned money and gave him a piano. (Harpsichords, of which you have read in the previous volume, were now fast going out, and pianos were becoming quite common.)

Schubert's Friendships

There is one thing you cannot help noticing when you read Schubert's life—the number of friends he made and the splendid way these stuck to him. You have just read how Spaun helped him, when he was a schoolboy, and now you will hear how a young man called Schober did the same. This Schober had come across some of Schubert's songs—in manuscript, for nothing of Schubert's was yet printed. He was so much struck with these that he called to see the young composer, and when he found that he was wasting his days in an occupation for which he was not fitted, he said to him 'Come and live with me, and I'll look after you.' The father was willing, so off the youth went, and now he could compose to his heart's content, instead of correcting short division sums or giving spelling lessons. Other friends gathered round him too, and tried to help him. One thing they felt really should be done was to print some of the lovely songs he had written. But they could not persuade any publisher to look at the work of an unknown youth, so in the end Schubert had to go on composing year after year and living one hardly knows how (for he could not stay very long with his friend Schober, as Schober had to take in a brother). And when he was twenty-five nothing was yet in print, so that his beautiful music, instead of being at the service of all the world, was known only to a few keen musicians in his own native city.

Now the father of one of Schubert's old friends of his school-days had a large house, and used to give fine concerts there of Schubert's music, so as to make it known, and the plan was hit upon of printing one of the best of the songs, having it sung at a concert, and then offering it for sale to the audience. The first song to be printed was the one which is now perhaps most famous—*The Erl King*. This was sung by one of Schubert's friends, who had a fine voice and a dramatic way of singing, and at once the people in the audience bought one hundred copies. This provided enough money to print another song, for the next concert, and so on! One reason why publishers would not undertake to bring out such a song as this was the difficulty of the piano part, which in *The Erl King* goes very fast and gives a wonderful feeling of a horseman galloping through a dark night and a ghostly enemy following swiftly after. You can get the song as a Gramophone record, and you will notice at once that it is quite as much a piano piece as a song. After hearing it you will be astonished to learn that Schubert wrote it in one afternoon.

Schubert's Songs

Schubert, from a boy upwards, took to song writing like a duck to water, and to instrumental writing (we may say) like a man to water. That is to say, song writing seemed natural to him, but instrumental writing he had to learn, as swimming has to be learnt. He wrote a lot of most beautiful instrumental works, but sometimes you feel (especially in a long piece) that he was not quite so much the complete master of this sort of composing as of the other.

If he got hold of a book of poems and opened it, at once he would seize on some verses, read them once or twice through, and see in a flash what was the best way to set them so as to bring out all the meaning and the feeling of the poet's words. Then he would sit down and write the music straight away.

There is a most lovely setting by him of Shakespeare's song, *Hark, hark, the lark.* It came about in this way. Schubert was walking in the country and saw a friend sitting at a table in an inn garden. He joined him, and took up the book he had been reading. It opened at *Cymbeline,* at the poem which Cloten's musicians perform to Imogen, to wake her sweetly in the morning—*Hark, hark, the lark.* 'Oh!' said Schubert, 'I have thought of such a lovely tune for that! What a pity I haven't some music-paper here!' The friend took up the bill of fare and drew some music lines on it with his pencil, and Schubert at once wrote that beautiful song that has now gone all through the world and is loved in every civilized country. (This song also you can get as a Gramophone record.) So quickly did Schubert write his songs that once or twice he actually forgot them again. On one occasion one of his friends put before him on the piano a manuscript song in the friend's own writing. Schubert played it through and said, 'That's not bad! Who composed it?' 'Why,' said the friend, 'you yourself did, and you gave it me a fortnight ago, but as it was too high for me I wrote it out afresh in another key.'

Altogether Schubert composed in his lifetime over 600 songs. As you have learnt, the publishers would at first not look at them. Later the tide turned, and the publishers became more willing. But they rarely gave him more than a few shillings for a song, and in spite of his genius he remained ever a poor man.

Instrumental Music

If you have not yet made acquaintance with Schubert's Piano Music (such as his *Impromptus,* and his *Moments Musicaux,* for instance), let us hope you may soon do so. Then there is some beautiful Chamber Music, and there are some Symphonies, of which two are most heard—the great C major Symphony and the one in B minor, of which only two movements exist, and which is therefore always called *The Unfinished Symphony.*

Schubert's Death

Like this symphony, Schubert's life itself was 'Unfinished'. If you will look back at the heading of this chapter, and see the dates there, you will realize that he only lived thirty-one years. It will strike you, too, that he died the year after Beethoven. For years Beethoven and Schubert had lived in the same city of Vienna, but

Beethoven was known to everyone, was admired, and had wealthy friends, whereas Schubert was known and loved only by a small circle of people, generally not so high in the social scale as those with whom Beethoven associated. So Beethoven knew nothing of Schubert and Schubert loved Beethoven at a distance. Then one day a friend took Schubert to visit Beethoven, but the younger man was so bashful that when the elder one asked him a question, instead of answering it on the writing-tablet held out to him (you remember, Beethoven was deaf), he caught up his hat and rushed to the door and bolted! Later he got more courage, and as for Beethoven, when he was shown some of the songs, he said, emphatically, 'Truly, Schubert has the divine gift in him!'

When Beethoven was dying Schubert visited him, and at the funeral he was one of the torch-bearers. On the way home he and the two friends who were with him stopped at an inn, and solemnly drank to the memory of the great man. Then they drank another solemn toast to the first of them who should follow him. This, as it turned out, was Schubert himself, who, weakly for many years, fell ill and died, lovingly cared for in the house of that elder brother, Ferdinand, who had been so kind to him from his boyhood. On his death-bed he was cheered by reading *The Last of the Mohicans* and other novels by the American novelist Fenimore Cooper, and a few days before he died he wrote to a friend asking him to lend him more books by the same author. He had begged to be buried near Beethoven, and his wish was fulfilled. In music he left over 1,000 compositions; in money— £2 10*s*. The stone placed over him has these words:

Music has here entombed a rich treasure—

But still fairer hopes.

QUESTIONS

*(To See Whether You Remember
the Chapter and Understand It)*

1. What was Schubert's nationality?

2. In what city did he spend his life?

3. What other great composers lived there in those days?

4. What was Schubert's father?

5. To what school was Schubert sent?

6. What instrument did he play in the family quartet?

7. How did he earn a living when he left school?

8. Was Schubert in your opinion a surly sort of fellow or a pleasant sort? Why do you think so?

9. Was he a slow, laborious composer, or a quick one? Can you remember any circumstances that will illustrate your answer?

10. Mention two or three of his songs and tell anything about how they were composed, or performed, or published.

11. Mention one or two Symphonies.

12. How old was Schubert when he died? Did he die poor or rich?

13. Tell anything you remember about Schubert's meetings with Beethoven.

14. Which of the two died first—Schubert or Beethoven?

THINGS TO DO

(For School and Home)

1. Get somebody to play you some of Schubert's music. Listen to it carefully and see if you really like it, and which pieces you like best, and why. Write down your opinion.

2. Next day get the same performer to play the pieces again, without your looking over them, and see if you can remember the name of each piece. Then look at what you wrote down yesterday and see if you still like the same pieces best.

3. If there are any parts you don't like, or seem not to understand, get the player to do them again, and look over the music so as to see how these parts are made up. Then listen again and see if you now understand better.

4. If you have a Pianola, Piano-player or Player-piano, get your parents to buy or borrow some Schubert rolls, and practise these yourself.

5. If you can play the Piano pretty well, ask your

teacher if there is any Schubert piece suitable for you.

6. If you know a Singer, get him or her to sing you some Schubert songs. Before each is sung, read the words through and understand them. Then listen to the song the first time just for its music, and the second time to see how the song-part and the piano-part express or set off the words. Then listen a third time just for the pleasure of it.

7. If you have a Gramophone, get hold of some Schubert song records, and of the records of *The Unfinished Symphony*. In listening to the Symphony, see if you can find places that illustrate what Schumann said about the Wind Instruments in Schubert's orchestration—'They chat with one another like human beings'.

8. If you have any of Schubert's music, write a preface to it, giving briefly the chief facts about the composer's life, and paste it on the back of the title-page.

9. Make up a little play about Schubert, write it out and act it with your companions.

10. Prepare a little lecture on Schubert, and give it, with musical illustrations by yourself and friends or by the Pianola or Gramophone.

JOHN FIELD

CHAPTER II

THE INVENTOR OF
THE NOCTURNE

JOHN FIELD

1782-1837

What is a Nocturne?

Before you begin to read this chapter play one of Chopin's Nocturnes, or get some one to play one to you. And as you play or hear it try to notice what it is like—what it is that makes a Nocturne a Nocturne, and not (say) a Minuet or a March.

The word 'Nocturne' means, of course, just a Night Piece—the sort of dreamy, tender music that might come into a composer's head as he stood looking over the fields or the sea on a starlight or moonlight night. But, besides suggesting this feeling, Chopin's Nocturnes, you will find, have also got other characteristics in common. Look, for instance, at the favourite one in E flat. You will notice that in the right hand we have a beautiful melody, that *floats,* as it were, on spreading waves of harmony in the left hand, which are made to sound on by the use of the sustaining pedal. Almost all the Chopin Nocturnes are like that, though the left-hand part is not in some of the Nocturnes so wave-like as in this Nocturne, whilst in others it is more so. This way of treating the two hands is really one of the 'distinguishing marks' of a Nocturne. If you were to make up a bit of slow melody, put to it a left-hand accompaniment of the sort described, and then play it to any one who knew anything about piano music, they would say at once, 'Why, that must be the beginning of some Nocturne.'

Who First Composed Such Pieces?

Now most people think the Chopin Nocturne style was invented by Chopin, but this was not so. An Irishman invented Chopin's Nocturnes for him, which, being a sort of 'bull', is just what an Irishman would do. This Irishman was John Field, and he was writing Nocturnes before Chopin was put into trousers. At one time everybody played his music, but now hardly anybody does so, and thus what he did for music is in danger of being forgotten.

Where and When Field was Born

Field was born in Dublin in 1782—that is to say, whilst Haydn was in his prime (how old was he?) and Beethoven a boy (and how old was *he*?). And he died in

1837, the year Queen Victoria came to the throne, when Schubert and Beethoven had been dead respectively nine and ten years, and Chopin and Schumann and Mendelssohn were all young men of twenty-seven or twenty-eight. That fixes him in his chronological place in your mind, I hope.

The Young Pianist

Field's father and grandfather lived together in Dublin and kept a sort of little school of music. The grandfather was an Organist and Pianist and the father played the fiddle in a theatre orchestra, and taught it to as many pupils as he could get. These two elder musicians gave the younger one (for Field had early taken to piano playing) many a good thrashing, thinking perhaps that they could whip music into him through the skin, instead of making him take it up gradually with the mind. Once the boy ran away from home to escape the whippings he got there, but he seems to have gone back again pretty soon.

At that time there was in Dublin a famous Italian pianist named Giordani (pronounce that 'Gee-or-daa-nee', saying the first two syllables quickly, which is as near as I can get to it in English spelling). To this man was young Field sent for lessons, and he got on so well that when he was nine his master made him appear at concerts, describing him on the bills as 'the much admired Master Field, a youth of eight years of age'. I am sorry to tell you that nearly all these youngsters who appear before the public are made out to be younger than they really are. When I visited Beethoven's birthplace at Bonn, I saw there a printed bill of his father's announcing the appearance at a concert on March 26, 1778, of his little son of 'six years'. You, who have read the account of Beethoven in my first volume, and know in what year he was born, can see what a shocking lie *that* was!

Field in London

When Field was eleven, his father left Dublin for Bath, and later went to London, where he became a member of the orchestra at the Haymarket Theatre. And in London the boy became pupil to a celebrated pianist of the day, that Clementi whose sonatinas you may know, and who was then the finest player in London. In 1794 young Field (this time 'aged ten') appeared in public, and old Haydn, who was in London just then, was in the audience and predicted that the boy would become a great musician.

Now Clementi was not only a player of pianos but also a maker of them, and he made Field spend a great deal of time in his piano shop, playing brilliant passages to customers, and showing off the instruments. Then when Clementi went abroad for the purposes of giving recitals and of selling pianos he took Field with him. When they got to St. Petersburg (which we now call Petrograd) Clementi opened a show-room for the pianos, and poor Field (aged nineteen, yet, as the great musician Spohr tells us, 'in an Eton suit which he had much outgrown') was kept at work displaying the qualities of the instruments.

When Clementi left Petrograd, Field remained behind, and a certain general took him in as his guest and introduced him into society. Soon he became very well known as a concert player, and had crowds of aristocratic pupils. Indeed he became so popular that he was spoilt, becoming lazy and frivolous. One of his pupils was Glinka, who became the founder of modern Russian music.

Field's Compositions

So long did Field live in Russia, and so connected with that country in people's minds did he become, that often he is spoken of in books as 'Russian Field'. He did a great deal of composition, and in 1814 composed his first Nocturnes. He also wrote Piano Sonatas and Concertos. The Concertos were for years very much played, and Schumann, in his time, praised them highly, but we never hear them now. Later, Field left Petrograd and lived in Moscow, and sometimes he travelled on recital tours. He played in London, and in Paris, and Florence, and Venice, and elsewhere, and the best judges of music were astonished at his playing, which was very simple and unaffected in style, and very neat and finished.

Field's Death

In Naples Field fell ill, and spent nine months in a hospital. A Russian nobleman found him there, and took him away with him. Gradually he was able to travel back to Russia with the nobleman, but there he fell ill again and died. The city of Moscow, recognizing what a great man he was, gave him a public funeral. His life was not a short one (fifty-five years), but probably it would have been longer and happier if he had not been so sternly treated as a boy at home, and then overworked in youth by Clementi. The result of this harshness seems to have been that when he got away from restraints, and was made much of in Russia, he 'lost his head' and became careless of his health and intemperate.

The Two Nocturne Writers

If possible get your teacher or some friend to play you not only the Chopin Nocturne I have mentioned (the one in E flat, Op. 9, No. 2), but also a certain one by Field in the same key (No. 1).

Field's begins:

And Chopin's begins:

If you listen to and look at those extracts carefully you will see how similar they are in style. But, of course, though we may *like* Field's piece, Chopin's is the one we *love*. Why? Because to Field's grace and beauty Chopin has added a deeper poetical feeling. It is as if I were to say to you (as the opening of a word-nocturne):

'The evening bell is ringing,
The cattle come home from the fields,'

and somebody were then to read to you Gray's 'Elegy', which begins with just this thought, but ever so much more beautifully expressed:

The curfew tolls the knell of parting day,
The lowing herd winds slowly o'er the lea.

But you see what Chopin learnt from Field, and if you will now look at and listen closely to the two Nocturnes you will see many others of Field's ideas that were adopted by Chopin, such as, for instance, this sort of ornamental, running, chromatic-scaly figure:

Field:

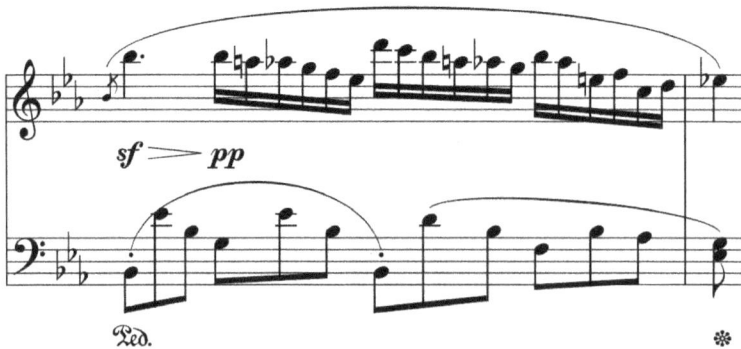

Chopin:

Then notice where Chopin got another of his charming little 'mannerisms', a turn followed by a high leap:

Field:

Chopin:

And so we could go on, comparing these and various other Field and Chopin Nocturnes.

But, since Field is little played to-day, why have I troubled to write a chapter about him? *Firstly,* because his Nocturnes, though not so deeply poetical as Chopin's, are refined and beautiful and worth more playing than they get. *Secondly,* because people so often forget what British composers have done for music, especially piano music, and they should be reminded of it. Look back again at Chapter II of *The First Book of the Great Musicians* and remind yourself of what the British composers did in laying the very *foundations* of keyboard music. Bach's Suites, we may say, are a building reared on the foundation laid by Bull and Byrd, and other British musicians, a century and more earlier. And, similarly, Chopin's Nocturnes are a building reared on the foundations laid by his elder contemporary, John Field.

QUESTIONS

*(To See Whether You Remember
the Chapter and Understand It)*

1. What is a Nocturne? Describe it as clearly as you can.

2. Where and when was Field born?

3. Where and when did he die?

4. What do you remember of Field's boyhood?

5. Mention one or two of Field's teachers.

6. How did Field come to be in Russia?

7. Tell anything you remember of his life there.

8. What did Field write besides his Nocturnes?

9. Mention a few things that Chopin learned from Field.

10. Why should we remember Field?

THINGS TO DO

These have already been mentioned in the chapter itself.

FELIX MENDELSSOHN

CHAPTER III

MENDELSSOHN

1809-1847

The Youth Who Could Do Everything

We will begin with a picnic in Wales, up amongst the hills. The engineer who is in charge of the mines of the district has had a tent carried up, and brought his family to celebrate his birthday among the miners. And with his family he has brought a guest who is staying with them, a young man from Germany, who has the reputation of being a good musician and who has been appearing at concerts in London. But this young man, it seems, is not only a musician. He throws himself into the fun and it really seems as though he can do everything. He can play all the games, or if there is one he cannot play, it has only to be explained to him and he understands it at once. He can sketch, and that quite beautifully. He can dance. In the evenings when they get home he can play chess and billiards and beat them all, he can ride and swim and is a great gymnast, and when he leaves this Welsh family and goes home they find that he can write the most interesting letters, describing all that he sees and does more like a practised author than a mere friendly letter-writer.

But it is the music he makes that pleases them most. He sees a creeping plant in the garden, with little blossoms almost the shape of trumpets. 'Fairy trumpets,' he says, and sits down and plays a piece on the piano— music for the fairies to play. Then he writes it out for one of the children, and draws all up the margin of the paper a sprig of the blossoms.

One morning as he is dressing he hears a boy of the family playing on the drawing-room piano a little tune he has made up in the Welsh style, and in the evening when the visitor sits down to play, out comes this very tune, turned into a long piece of beautiful music.

When they are out in the grounds one evening the young man says, 'What a pity we haven't an instrument out here!' One of the boys rushes to the gardener's cottage and borrows a fiddle. It is a wretched old thing, and all the strings are snapped but one. The young man bursts into fits of laughter when he sees such an instrument, but he takes it, and somehow he draws beautiful music out of that one string, to which his companions listen eagerly until darkness comes and it is time to go in.

That is Mendelssohn 'all over'—the youth to whom everything came easily and who was nearly always in high spirits.

The Boyhood

Mendelssohn had had a wonderful musical boyhood. He learnt early to play the Piano, and from nine onwards appeared in concerts; he learnt the Violin too, and did a great deal of composition; and he sang alto in the great choral society of Berlin, his native place, 'standing amongst the grown-up people in his child's dress, a tight-fitting jacket cut very low at the neck, over which the trousers were buttoned, into the slanting pockets of these the little fellow liked to thrust his hands, rocking his curly head from side to side, and shifting restlessly from one foot to the other.'

When he was twelve he began to compose more systematically, copying all his pieces into a big album, and, when that was finished, starting another, until, at the end of his life, there were forty-four of these volumes on his shelves—one for each year and a few over.

Sunday Music

Mendelssohn's parents were rich and had a large and beautiful house, with a big dining-room, where every other Sunday they gave concerts for their friends. The children took a great part in the music. Felix, of whom I have been telling you these things, often composed some of the music, and conducted the Orchestra, standing on a stool; Fanny, his clever sister, played the Piano, Rebecka sang, and Paul played the 'Cello. This is the very best way of making music, and more families could do it if they tried, though not all could do it on so big a scale, or do it so well as to be worth their friends' frequent hearing. And of course not all families could provide their own domestic composer.

The Mendelssohn family's music-making was so famous that any notable musicians who passed through Berlin were glad to be present to hear it.

Some Holiday Music

The Mendelssohns lived in music, and when they went on holiday they did not leave it behind. When Felix was fourteen he and his two brothers were taken on a tour in Silesia by their father. At one town a Charity Concert was being prepared, and the committee asked if they might announce that Felix would play a Mozart Concerto with their Orchestra. But at the rehearsal the Orchestra played so much out of tune and out of time that Felix made the schoolmaster go on to the platform and say that, instead of playing the Concerto, Master Mendelssohn would extemporize, and this was done, Felix playing a brilliant improvisation on some tunes out of works by Mozart and Weber.

When they went to the seaside next year they found that there was a wind band there, so Felix wrote for it an Overture, which the band played and which he afterwards published.

The 'Midsummer Night's Dream' Overture

When he was seventeen-and-a-half Mendelssohn wrote a most beautiful overture, intended to precede Shakespeare's *A Midsummer Night's Dream*. To this day, this is the music we generally hear in a London theatre when they perform the play, and to the end of his life the composer never composed anything finer. Its opening is very light and fairy-like, so that somebody has said that Mendelssohn was 'the first composer to bring the fairies into the orchestra.' But there are others besides fairies in Shakespeare's play and so there are in Mendelssohn's overture to it; at one place you can distinctly hear Bottom's 'Hee-haw'.

Mendelssohn later wrote other music for *A Midsummer Night's Dream*—for instance, the famous Wedding March, which is nowadays as much used at church weddings as at stage weddings. And there is also a very beautiful soft Night Piece, or 'Notturno'.

Other Orchestral Pieces

Mendelssohn is famous for his Overtures, some of which were not intended for plays, but just as orchestral pieces to begin a concert. Indeed he may be said to have invented the Concert Overture, writing it much on the lines of the first movement of a Beethoven symphony. One of the best of these concert overtures is the *Hebrides Overture,* sometimes called *Fingal's Cave.* When Mendelssohn was travelling in Scotland, of which country he was very fond, he visited that cave, and there came to his mind a beautiful bit of music, which he wrote down and afterwards used as the opening of this Overture. Some other orchestral works of Mendelssohn are in the form of full symphonies. He gave these names: there are a *Scotch Symphony* and an *Italian Symphony* (in which some of his feelings during his tours in Scotland and Italy are reproduced), and a *Reformation Symphony* with the finale made out of the fine old tune which you will find in all Hymn Tune books to Luther's hymn, 'A Safe Stronghold our God is still'.

Pieces for orchestra and a solo instrument are the very popular Violin Concerto and the two Piano Concertos.

There is also a good deal of Chamber Music.

Mendelssohn's Oratorios

Besides the pieces just mentioned, Mendelssohn wrote a good deal of choral music, and especially sacred music, such as settings of the Psalms, and some Oratorios—*St. Paul, Elijah,* and the *Hymn of Praise.*

The first performance of *Elijah* was at Birmingham, so English people heard it before Mendelssohn's own countrymen. Mendelssohn himself conducted and was delighted with the solo singers and the chorus and the orchestra, and with the audience, too. He wrote home to his brother saying, 'No work of mine ever went so admirably at the first performance, or was received with such enthusiasm as this. I never in my life heard a better performance, no, nor so good, and almost doubt if I shall ever hear one like it again.'

The Piano Music

Mendelssohn was himself a fine pianist, so naturally he wrote a good deal of piano music. Amongst this there is a *Rondo Capriccioso* that you may have heard (you know what a Rondo is, and a Capriccioso piece is naturally one that cuts jolly 'capers'). And you must know some of the *Songs without Words*. The idea of these, of course, is a beautiful tune, of a song kind, with an accompaniment to it going on all the time. And there are other pieces, but these are perhaps the best known. At first nobody in England would buy the *Songs without Words*, and when Mendelssohn, being in London, went to Novello's shop to see how much money they had for him from the proceeds of the first book of six of the pieces he found that they had only sold about a hundred copies in four years and had only a pound or two for him. Afterwards people became even too fond of these pieces, so that every home in England where there was a piano had the full set of them, and other good music was in some cases neglected.

Mendelssohn as Pianist

There must be many young pianists amongst the readers of this book, and they may care to have a description of Mendelssohn's playing, which was very famous.

He was a good sight reader and could play at once anything you put before him. And he was a good memory player, and hardly ever used printed music except when he was sight reading. Train yourself in sight reading and memory playing by all means! And, once his boyhood was past, he *never practised.* But in this you and I cannot, I fear, afford to follow his example—can we? Madame Schumann said that Mendelssohn's playing was one of the most delightful things she had ever heard in her life. She said 'in hearing him one forgot the *player* and only revelled in the full enjoyment of the *music.*'

Joachim said that Mendelssohn's playing in a *staccato* passage was 'the most extraordinary thing possible, for life and crispness.' He had great 'fire' in his playing, yet great delicacy, and he must have listened and trained himself to get very good tone, because in the softest passages everything could be clearly heard, even in the largest hall, whilst in the loudest passages the effect was never harsh. It is in the tone they produce that many well-known players of to-day fail. Mendelssohn's phrasing was beautifully clear, and he used the sustaining pedal with great thoughtfulness. '*Strict time was one of his hobbies.*'

Mendelssohn as Organist

As an organist, too, Mendelssohn was celebrated. Whenever he came to England he had to play on all the greatest organs. He had written six fine Organ Sonatas, which you can often hear nowadays at recitals, and he was very fond of playing Bach's organ fugues, and did a great deal to make these popular amongst English organists. But one thing he could not do that you or I could probably do quite well. After a church service he could not 'play the people out,' and once at St. Paul's Cathedral, when the organist got him to play a concluding voluntary, as the congregation did not go, the vergers, who wanted to get home to dinner, went to the organ-blower and made him leave his work, so that the playing came to a sudden end in the middle of a bar, and the people quickly dispersed.

Mendelssohn and Bach

You have read about Bach in *The First Book of the Great Musicians.* After his death, the style of music changed for a time; Fugues and Suites went out and Sonatas and Symphonies came in. And old Bach was almost forgotten, and whilst his sons lived their music was more thought of than his. Then came Haydn and Mozart and Beethoven, and so people went on forgetting old Bach. It was Mendelssohn who did more than any one else to bring Bach to life again. As a youth of eighteen he prepared a choir in the great *St. Matthew Passion,* and gave the first performance of this that had taken place since Bach died, over seventy years before. We owe him a great debt for making us realize the beauty of Bach, as we do also an English organist who did much the same here—Samuel Wesley.

Mendelssohn and an English Composer

Another thing we owe to Mendelssohn is the discovery of Sterndale Bennett. When Mendelssohn first started coming to this country British people had an idea that no Briton could compose fine music. But Mendelssohn went to a concert at the Royal Academy of Music, heard a student, Bennett, play some of his own music, and was so much struck with his compositions that he invited him to Germany and made much of him there, as did other great German musicians, such as Schumann. Then the English musicians, seeing one of their young countrymen taken up in musical Germany, thought there must be something in him, and so gave him a chance in his own country. And so gradually people awoke to the fact that one can be an Englishman and at the same time a composer. Sterndale Bennett wrote some fine music (a little in Mendelssohn's style) and then, unfortunately, left off composing in middle life, so that he never came to his full development. But, all the same, with him the tide of British music turned. *Thank you, Mendelssohn!*

QUESTIONS

*(To See Whether You Remember
the Chapter and Understand It)*

1. Tell anything you remember showing what sort of a youth Mendelssohn was.

2. Were his family musical? If so, tell anything you remember about their musical doings.

3. What do you remember about some music Mendelssohn wrote for a certain Shakespeare play?

4. Mention the names of any other Orchestral pieces by Mendelssohn, and say what you remember about them.

5. What Oratorios did Mendelssohn write?

6. And what Piano music?

7. What do you know about his Piano playing?

8. And his Organ playing?

9. What did he do for Bach?

10. And what for British music?

THINGS TO DO

1. Get the *Midsummer Night's Dream* Overture as a Gramophone record, or a piano piece, and listen to it carefully to see what there is in it, and how it is made

up. If you get the Gramophone record, try to find out, by listening carefully, which instruments are playing the different bits. Get the *Notturno* also.

2. Play, or get somebody to play to you, some of the *Songs without Words,* and then study them to find out how they are made. Do the same with any others of the piano pieces.

3. Get Gramophone records of some of Mendelssohn's Chamber Music, and study it until you know it thoroughly.

4. Get somebody to sing you parts of *Elijah*, or else get these for the Gramophone. Look at a copy of the Piano Score, and find out where in the story of *Elijah* comes each song that you hear.

5. Get a friendly church organist to play you one of Mendelssohn's Organ Sonatas—several times, so that you can study it, and remember it. It will help you if the organist will play the chief bits first, and explain to you how Mendelssohn has worked them up into his 'movements'.

6. There is a favourite Christmas Hymn Tune of yours which is adapted from a work of Mendelssohn's. Look through a Hymn Tune book and find out what it is.

7. Get a Violinist and Pianist to play you part of the Violin Concerto, or get the Gramophone record of one of the movements of this.

CHAPTER IV

ABOUT THE OLD MIRACLE PLAYS AND MASQUES, AND WHAT SPRANG FROM THEM

Where Opera Comes From

This chapter is written to show the origin of Opera. In the first volume there was a short description of Opera. Where does Opera come from? It comes from a human instinct, or rather two or three human instincts—

(1) the instinct to Sing,

(2) the instinct to Act,

(3) the instinct to Dance.

As long as men have been in the world they have felt these three instincts leading them to make Songs and Plays about what interests them, and also to express their jollity, or sometimes their sorrow, by moving rhythmically to music. When you have the singing and acting combined you have OPERA, and many Operas have also dancing in them, which dancing we call BALLET (pronounce *Bal*-ay).

Miracle Plays — A Visit to Chester in 1500

Imagine yourself in some English city at the time of the year when the great plays are performed—say Chester, in Whitsun week, about 1500. These plays are intended to teach the people about religion. At Chester there are, at the date mentioned, twenty-four of the plays, all performed on one day, and the custom of performing them goes back for at least three centuries earlier.

Each play is performed by the men of some particular trade; for instance, the Drapers play the *Creation,* the Water-drawers of the Dee (appropriately) *The Ark and the Flood,* the Barbers and Candle-makers *The Story of Lot and Abraham,* and so on, until we enter the New Testament with *The Birth of Christ,* played by the Slaters, and end it with the Weavers' play of *The Last Judgement.* And thus, in one day, we have gone through the main events of the whole Bible.

Each of these trades has its own Pageant Stage on wheels, and its own simple scenery and very gay dresses. The Drapers will give their play in a certain street, and then move to another street and give it again. Meanwhile the Tanners will come to the place where the Drapers were, and so on—so that all over the city of Chester the people who live in any particular district have each one of the plays brought, as it were, to their very door.

This is to prevent overcrowding in any one spot. And lest there should be disturbances the Mayor has issued a proclamation that whilst the plays are going on nobody is to wear weapons in the city of Chester, on pain of imprisonment by the Mayor, fine by the King, and cursing by the Pope, which is a pretty fearsome combination of punishments. So now all is ready and we will watch just one of these plays. Let us choose the Water-drawers' play of *The Ark and the Flood.*

The Noah's Ark Play

Up comes, with a merry crowd, the Water-drawers' pageant-stage, or pageant-cart, and the play begins. The first character to speak is God. He tells Noah that there is to be a flood, warns him to prepare the Ark and tells him just how to make it, and what animals to put into it.

Then out speaks Shem and says he's got a good sharp axe and will help his father to make the Ark. Ham says he's got the sharpest hatchet in the town, and will do his part too, Japhet says he can make wooden pins, and with his hammer knock them in, and Noah's wife says she will go and gather timber. Shem's wife fetches a block on which they can work the wood with their tools, and Ham's wife has the good idea of going off to get clay to fill up the cracks in the Ark when it is ready for caulking. Japhet's wife gathers the chips from the work and makes it her business to cook dinner for the workers. So very quickly they are all busy.

Then Noah makes a long speech and you will see how quickly a Stage Ark can be made, for by the time he has finished his speech the Ark is finished too.

> Now in the name of God I will begin,
> To make the ship that we shall in,
> That we be ready for to swim,
> At the coming of the flood.
> These boards I join together,
> To keep us safe from the weather,
> That we may roam both hither and thither
> And safe be from this flood.
> Of this tree I will have the mast,
> Tied with cables that will last,
> With a sail yard for each blast
> And each thing in its kind.
>   With topmast high and bowsprit,
> With cords and ropes I hold all fit
> To sail forth at the next weete [tide].
> This ship is at an end.
> Wife, in this castle we shall be kept:
> My children and thou I would in leapt!

But now comes a difficulty, and, as you will soon see, the Monk, or whoever it was who wrote that play, has brought it in just to cheer the audience with a little fun. When they begin to go into the Ark Noah's wife will not budge. In vain poor old Noah says, 'Good wife, do as I bid.' All the animals are supposed to be driven in (Noah's sons have pictures on parchment of cats and dogs, and foxes and hares, and herons and rooks, and lions and leopards, and as each is supposed to be entering they say its name). At last all is ready, and the water is supposed to be rising, but still the silly old woman stays on shore and refuses to join the family unless she can bring with her her 'gossips', or friends. They all try to persuade her, and Japhet cries:

> Mother, we pray you all together,
> For we are here, your children
> Come into the ship for fear of the weather.

In the end they have to put the old lady in by main force, and you may be sure they do it in such a way as to give the spectators a good laugh.

Then the windows of the Ark are shut up and you hear Noah sing a Psalm in Latin, *Salva me, Domine!* At the end of the Psalm you are to suppose forty days have passed, and you see Noah send out a raven, which never returns, and then a dove. When the dove has gone they have another one ready with an olive branch in its mouth, which they let down by string (a stuffed dove, or a wooden one, perhaps, but supposed to be the first one come back), and Noah takes it in, and so the play goes on until at last it ends with a long speech by God, and the words:

> My blessing now I give thee here,
> To thee Noah, my servant dear;
> For vengeance shall no more appear;
> And now farewell, my darling dear!

So that is how our ancestors amused themselves and taught the scripture stories at Whitsuntide; and at Christmas and Easter and on Corpus Christi day there were other plays suited to the season. You can get some of the Chester, Wakefield, Coventry, and York plays, and the Cornish Mystery-Play of the Three Maries, and the old play, *Everyman*, and similar things quite cheaply in the 'Everyman Library', if you want. You will find that some of them have more music in them than the one I have described. For instance, the Coventry Christmas Play has the song of the Angels, and songs by the Shepherds, and a Lullaby by the mothers of the Innocents. Plays of this kind were not only common in England but all over Europe, and we may fairly see in them the origin of:

(a) our Drama—that is, plays without music,

(b) our Opera—that is, plays set to music,

(c) our Oratorio—that is, sacred plays with music but not acting (and therefore, really, plays no longer).

The Masques

Another form of entertainment the influence of which we see in Opera is the Masque. The Miracle Plays were for the common people, the Masques for the rich nobles. The Masque was a sort of private theatricals, popular in the sixteenth and early seventeenth centuries. It first came about by people introducing into festive processions men wearing masks, who represented allegorical personages, such as Virtue, or Vice, and acted in dumb show. Then it became more elaborate, and turned into a sort of play of an allegorical kind.

Very often a wedding was celebrated with a Masque after the feast, and so was a royal visit to any great house. For instance, when Queen Elizabeth went in state once to visit the lawyers of Gray's Inn, in London, they entertained her with a Masque.

A Seventeenth-Century London Masque

Next time you go down Whitehall have a good look at the Banqueting House, which is now a naval museum (you can go in for sixpence). This is the building from which Charles I stepped out on to the scaffold (which was erected in front of it), and before that time it had been the scene of many events. For instance, in 1613 there was a famous Masque performed there to celebrate the marriage of the Earl of Somerset and Lady Frances Howard. In the upper room, which you can still see, they put up pillars and platforms, and a triumphal arch in front of these. They had a painted canvas sky above the platform, and on each side of it a high promontory with three big golden pillars. Between the promontories was what appeared to be the sea, with ships, some just painted on the background and others made to move. In front of the sea was a beautiful garden, where the masquers were.

The King and Queen and Prince were present, and after the trumpets had blown and they had entered and taken their seats in the audience, the Masque began with four Squires approaching them and explaining what was about to befall. At the end of these four speeches appeared Error, 'in a skin coat scaled like a serpent,' and Rumour, 'in a skin coat full of winged tongues,' and Curiosity, 'in a skin coat full of eyes,' and Credulity, 'in a like habit painted with ears.'

When these had acted awhile there came in the Four Winds, the East Wind 'in a skin coat of the colour of the sun-rising,' the Northern Wind 'in a grisled skin coat of hair,' and so on. All these Winds had wings on their shoulders and feet.

Then came in the Four Elements: Earth, in a coat grass-green, a mantle painted with plants and flowers, 'and on his head an oak growing'; Water, in a coat 'waved, with a mantle full of fishes, on his head a dolphin'; Air, in a sky-coloured coat, with birds on his mantle, and an eagle on his head; and Fire, with a flame-coloured mantle, and on his head a salamander. Then came the Four Continents, suitably dressed, and the Three Destinies, and at last Harmony, with nine musicians with garlands, playing and singing.

Then followed a great deal of dancing, and solo singing and chorus singing, and at the end the Four Squires came on again and wished the newly married couple happiness, and the people on the stage got into boats and sailed away, whilst a song was sung.

That gives you a sort of rough idea of a Masque. Shakespeare sometimes introduced Masques and Masquers into his plays (for instance, in *The Tempest* there is a Masque to celebrate the engagement of Miranda and Ferdinand). Milton wrote the most famous Masque of all, *Comus*.

QUESTIONS

*(To See Whether You Remember
the Chapter and Understand It)*

1. Describe, as well as you can, what Miracle Plays were.

2. Do the same for Masques.

3. What is a Ballet?

4. What three human instincts come out in Opera?

THINGS TO DO

A good Christmas entertainment would be a Play made out of the Christmas Miracle Plays. In the Wakefield Second Nativity Play (in the volume mentioned on page 44) there is a very funny part about one of the shepherds who steals a sheep belonging to another shepherd, carries it home, puts it in a cradle, and pretends it is a new baby. Don't leave this bit out if you act the play. The Coventry play has rather more opportunity for music, and I do not see why a class of children should not, amongst them, make up tunes for the songs. Or a good play could be made by taking parts of each of these plays. Instrumental music for the Shepherds' Watch, or for the overture, could be taken from *Messiah,* and parts of Bach's *Christmas Oratorio* might come in. But, of course, an ambitious class with an intelligent teacher could do things in a more 'authentic' way than this—giving one of the plays as it stands, and composing the music, with or without the help of the best musician in the neighbourhood.

CHAPTER V

ABOUT ORATORIOS

What is an Oratorio?

An Oratorio is a long sacred piece, with vocal solos and choruses and instrumental music, and generally it tells a story, which is often taken from the Bible. Handel's *Messiah* is an Oratorio, and so is Bach's *Passion according to St. Matthew,* and so are Haydn's *Creation* and Mendelssohn's *Elijah,* and Elgar's *Apostles* and *The Kingdom.* In all those works the story told comes from the Bible. In Elgar's oratorio, *Gerontius,* a story is also told, and a very beautiful one, but here the story comes not from the Bible but from a modern poem describing the death and after-death of a saint of the Church.

The First Oratorios

It is always difficult to say what was 'the first' of anything, but the first pieces to which the name 'Oratorio' was given were some which were performed in Rome in the sixteenth century, by a very good priest, who has been canonized by the Roman Catholic Church and is called St. Philip Neri (pronounce *Nay*-ree). You must know about him, for he was a great man.

49

ST. PHILIP NERI

Neri was born in Florence in 1515, and his father was a lawyer. He did so much good even as a boy that everybody called him 'The Good Pippo' ('short' for Philip). A very rich man, his uncle, wanted to make him his heir, but Philip refused, and when he was eighteen decided to go to Rome, and to put aside all thoughts of worldly success. When he got there he found a gentleman from his own native city, who gave him a small room and a daily allowance of meal of which to make his food. He spent his time in visiting the poor and sick, and in prayer. This went on for a long time, but when he was thirty-six he was persuaded to become a priest. He then started a sort of prayer-chapel or oratory, which he built on the roof of his church. A great many young men, many of them rich, used to come to his daily meetings.

Philip wanted to make religion attractive to the boys and young men, so he started the acting of religious plays, with music. These were called Oratorios, because they took place in the Oratory. Later Philip built a larger church in another part of Rome, and his Oratorios here became very popular and famous. Before Philip's time, and in Italy as in England, there had been religious 'Miracle Plays' and 'Mysteries', and some of them had a little music. But Philip's were very notable.

Philip died in 1595, and five years later a composer in Rome, CAVALEIRI (Cav-al-ee-*ay*-ree), composed a piece of something the same kind, but set to music throughout, and with scenery, acting, solo and chorus singing, instrumental music, and even dancing (Philip had sometimes had dancing—dancing not being in those days a mere amusement, as it generally is to-day). Cavalieri's oratorio was called *The Representation of the Soul and the Body,* and the characters in it were Time, Life, The World, Pleasure, Intellect, The Soul, and The Body. This was performed in 1600, and is generally considered the foundation-stone of the modern Oratorio, but the acting part was dropped by composers who followed Cavalieri, and to-day we do not have acting in an Oratorio as a rule, nor even scenery.

Passion Music

In Germany and elsewhere another sort of piece had come into existence, which was also a kind of Oratorio. In Holy Week the clergy would hold services for the singing of the story of the Passion of Christ, taken from one of the Gospels. They would have one singer, called the Evangelist, who would sing all the Narrative parts, and another for Christ, who would sing all the words of Christ when they came into the narrative, and another called the Crowd, who would sing such words as 'Crucify him!', or other words spoken by the body of people present in the story. By and by skilled composers took up this form of music and made it more elaborate. One of the greatest of these was the German composer Schütz, who was born exactly a hundred years before Bach.

When Bach himself arrived he became the very greatest composer of Passion Music there has ever been. He wrote five settings of the Passion, and of these three remain to-day—those according to St. Luke, St. John, and St. Matthew. The last is much the finest, and you can hear it in most large towns every year, in Holy Week. It is one of the greatest pieces of music ever composed. Bach has a Narrator (whom, he, also, calls 'The Evangelist'), another singer for Jesus, another for Peter, another for the High Priest, and so on. The Choir takes the part of the Crowd, and both certain soloists and the choir have some pieces of musical meditation (so to speak) on each little bit of the story as it is told.

Amongst the meditations are verses of hymns, very finely set by Bach to the old German hymn-tunes, or Chorales, with beautifully flowing alto and tenor and bass parts and lovely harmonies.

Another work of Bach's is *The Christmas Oratorio*, and he wrote about 200 Church Cantatas, which are something between a big Anthem and a small Oratorio.

Handel's Oratorios

Handel, who, as you remember, lived at exactly the same period as Bach (both born in 1685), wrote a great many fine oratorios. They were written in England, for the English people, and were very popular here, but of late years they have been much less performed—all except our favourite Christmas piece, *Messiah*, which, happily, still goes on.

Here are the names of some of Handel's Oratorios:

Saul (from which comes the solemn *Dead March*, played by the band at military funerals, and by organists at funeral services in church).

Theodora (from which comes the lovely song, 'Angels, ever bright and fair').

Samson.

Judas Maccabaeus (an Oratorio all about fighting).

Israel in Egypt (which has a 'Hailstone Chorus', and music for the Plague of Frogs, and other descriptive things, and also very fine double choruses, i.e. choruses for two choirs singing together).

Haydn's 'Creation'

A little later than Handel we get Haydn. When he came to England and heard Handel's Oratorios here, and especially *Messiah,* he said he felt that he, too, would like to write an Oratorio, and *The Creation* is the result. It has fine choruses in it, such as 'The Heavens are Telling', and beautiful solo tunes, such as 'With Verdure clad'. When it was finished some enthusiastic Austrian noblemen arranged a performance, paid all expenses, and gave Haydn the money taken at the doors, which was over £300. When Haydn first heard it performed (at Vienna in 1799) he was so excited that he said, 'One moment I was as cold as ice, and the next I seemed on fire.'

The Creation has been very popular in England, and is still often to be heard, though not so often as formerly.

Mendelssohn's Oratorios

In a previous chapter something has been said about Mendelssohn's Oratorios. The greatest is *Elijah,* which tells its story very vividly. Many of the solos from *Elijah,* such as 'O rest in the Lord', are known to almost everybody, everywhere.

Elgar's Oratorios

These have already been spoken of. *The Apostles* tells the story of Christ's choosing of his twelve Apostles, and the doings of Christ and of them, the betrayal of Christ by Judas, and the Crucifixion, Resurrection, and Ascension. *The Kingdom* takes the story forward with the doings of the Disciples after Christ had left them.

Gerontius, or, in full, *The Dream of Gerontius,* is a setting of a very beautiful poem by Cardinal Newman.

Besides these there are a great many other Oratorios by composers British, and American, and foreign, but those mentioned are the chief Oratorios that you are likely to have a chance of hearing.

QUESTIONS

*(To See Whether You Remember
the Chapter and Understand It)*

1. How would you describe an Oratorio?

2. Tell, in your own words, what you know of St. Philip Neri.

3. How was Cavalieri's Oratorio *Soul and Body* different from Oratorios to-day?

4. Describe Passion Music, and mention the chief writers of it.

5. Which is the finest 'Passion' ever written?

6. Give the names of four or five of the most important of Handel's Oratorios.

7. And the name of one of Haydn's.

8. And the name of the most popular Oratorio by Mendelssohn.

9. And the names of three by Elgar. Tell anything you know about these.

THINGS TO DO

1. Get Mendelssohn's *Elijah,* or Handel's *Messiah,* or Haydn's *Creation* and look through the words at the beginning (they are generally printed out in full, before the music begins).

2. Then play, or get some one to play, some parts of the Oratorio, such as the Overture and some of the choruses and solos. Or get Gramophone records of these. Try to get a pretty good idea of what the Oratorio is about, and how the composer has treated his subject.

3. Get somebody to sing (or play) you some of the best bits of Bach's *Christmas Oratorio* (such as the Cradle Song).

4. And also some of the Chorales or Hymn Tunes in the *St. Matthew Passion* (notice the flowing voice parts in these).

5. If you can get somebody to play you parts of an Elgar Oratorio, so much the better. You can enjoy a few things as Gramophone records if you are rich and intelligent—and I hope you are both!

CHAPTER VI

THE EARLIEST OPERAS

ONE of the greatest dates in history is 1453, the date when the Eastern Empire fell and the Turks took Constantinople. You may wonder what that has to do with music, but you will soon see.

The Renaissance

Constantinople had been a great centre of scholarship. Many learned and studious Greeks were living there, and there were great collections of Greek literature and art. When the Turks entered the city the Greeks fled, and took with them such of their ancient manuscripts as they could carry. Wherever they could find a wealthy patron to support them they settled, and so the study of the ancient Greek language and literature was spread over Europe, and, as a result, the very thought of Europe was changed. This change of thought is called by a word meaning 'Re-birth'—RENAISSANCE (or RENASCENCE). The new ideas which sprang out of the revival of the old ones altered men's views on Politics and Religion and science, changed the course of Literature, and brought in a new Architecture based on that of ancient Greece.

It will give you a rough but sufficient idea of the change in Architecture if you think first of Westminster Abbey, and then of St. Paul's Cathedral. The Abbey, with its pointed arches, and interlacing lines, and slender columns, belongs to the older style of mediaeval architecture; the Cathedral, with its massive blocks of masonry, its great round arches, its pillared portico, and its dome, illustrates the Renaissance style, which is based on that of the ancient Greek temples.

In the Abbey you feel a sense of awe and mystery that you do not feel in the Cathedral, where everything is much more open and simple in style. The Abbey, we may say, is graceful and mysterious, the Cathedral massive and striking. It is worth while to look at some pictures of these great churches, if you have them, and think out what has just been said, because it will, in a moment, illustrate a similar change that the Renaissance a little later brought about in music.

What Happened at Florence

As Italy was so much nearer to the East than Germany or France or Britain, of course a great many Greek scholars settled there, and Florence, in particular, became a great centre for the study of the Greek language and literature, and art, for in Florence there long lived a great and rich family called the Medici family (pronounce Med-*ee*-chee) who made their palace a meeting-place for learned and cultured men of every kind, and there were other palaces, of other families who followed the Medici fashion, and monasteries, too, where the studies went on very actively.

58

The Renaissance in Music

One little group of learned men used to gather at the palace of a Count Bardi at the end of the sixteenth century (a century and a half after the Renaissance had begun). They discussed the Greek plays and Greek music, and wondered if these could be revived, and at last one of them, Vincenzo Galilei (father of Galileo Galilei, the great astronomer), wrote a piece modelled on what, from his reading of the Greek classics, he imagined to be the Greek style. The idea was, instead of the elaborate madrigal style of which you read in the first volume of this book, and which was at its height just then, to have a single voice, declaiming rather than singing, and to support it with a few chords on Lutes or similar instruments.

Other composers took up this idea, and by and by real Operas were composed, chiefly treated in this way (dialogue supported by chords), but with bits of simple chorus (also largely in plain chords), and with an orchestra of any instruments that were to be had, used both to accompany the voices and also to play little bits of music in between the vocal parts. A line of one of these earliest operas will show you the style of thing.

Io   che d'al - ti sos - pir vaga   e   di pian - - ti,

(Free translation: I, that from above breathe plaints and sighs.)

There you see the voice part imitating the speaking voice rather than singing a tune, and under it a plain accompaniment of chords.

Generally the Operas of this time were on subjects taken from Greek mythology. For instance, the story of Orpheus and how he went down to the place of death to bring back his Eurydice, was used. So altogether the early operas were very much influenced by the study of Greek thought, and the invention of Opera may fairly be considered one of the results of the Renaissance.

The Old Style and the New

If you will look at that little bit of music, made out of plain chords, one after another, and compare it with a bit of a song with lute accompaniment belonging to the same period, you will see what the difference amounts to.

Be still, for if you ev-er do the like

Here you will see how the lute player, instead of playing mere chords (i.e. just 'Harmony'), weaves a combination of melodies (i.e. 'Counterpoint').

Now let us look at the same sort of thing in a three-part chorus. Here is a bit of one of the new Florentine works—

And here is a bit of one of the older style pieces—

Again you see just the same difference. The newer style of piece is in chunks of harmony, and the older style of piece is a weaving together of counterpoint.

Both these styles of writing were going on at the same time. The older-minded composers sometimes had 'chunks', and the newer ones tended more and more to fall back into the 'weaving' process. But you see the difference, and you will realize that these new Opera and Oratorio composers brought about a new way of looking at music—as we may say, a *perpendicular* way instead of the old *horizontal* way. After a time composers learnt more and more to look at music in both ways together.

If you recall any music you heard in illustration of the Elizabethan Composers (Volume I, chapter II) you will remember that it was nearly all *horizontal*. And if you then recall any of the Purcell music you heard (Volume I, chapter III) you will remember that some of it was *perpendicular* or 'chunky' (for instance any Recitatives and some parts of the Choruses) whilst other parts were *horizontal,* or woven. But even when composers wrote horizontally they now had a clear idea of the chords they were using; in other words, they were writing both horizontally and perpendicularly at the same time.

Frozen Music

Now let us look at some Architecture. Somebody has called Architecture 'Frozen Music', and it is true that there are lots of things in Architecture that remind us of Music. If you glance at the picture opposite you will see a bit of old-style (early Gothic) 'frozen music'—Counterpoint, etc., woven lines. Now if you will look below you will see also a bit of new-style (or 'Renaissance') 'frozen music'—Harmony, one thing just above or against another, architectural 'chords' as it were.

Remember as much of this chapter as you can. It tries to give you, in a rough-and-ready sort of way, an idea of the beginnings of Opera, and then to show you in what sort of style the early Opera writers composed.

COUNTERPOINT IN ARCHITECTURE

HARMONY IN ARCHITECTURE

QUESTIONS

*(To See Whether You Remember
the Chapter and Understand It)*

1. When were the first Operas written?

2. And where?

3. What was the chief idea of their writers, i.e. what were they trying to do?

4. What sort of music did they write, and how was it different from what went before?

5. Why is Westminster Abbey like an Anthem of Queen Elizabeth's day, and St. Paul's like some of the Anthems of Charles the Second's time? It is rather difficult to put this into words, but you might try.

THINGS TO DO

There are none—unless perhaps you were to get hold of a Gramophone record of one of Purcell's or Handel's or Mendelssohn's Recitatives, and see how the speaking style of song, supported by chords, was still going on long after those people in Florence invented it. Also if you cared you could put on the Gramophone a record of some Handel chorus and notice whether the composer has written it in *(a)* the Harmonic style, or *(b)* the Contrapuntal style, or *(c)* sometimes a bit in one and sometimes a bit in the other (the 'Hallelujah Chorus' is a good example of the mixed styles).

CHAPTER VII

MORE ABOUT OPERA

If You Were Writing an Opera

If you were writing an Opera which should you consider more important—the play or the music? Just think a moment. Suppose we imagine a school opera. Let us make up a plot. How would this do—taken from *Tom Brown's Schooldays?*

ACT I. SCENES 1 AND 2.

The Head, distressed that Tom Brown is always in mischief, hits on a good idea—to put a young and nervous new boy into his study and in his charge, so that he will feel a sense of responsibility. On the first day of term he invites Tom to tea and introduces him to Arthur, the new boy.

ACT II.

Tom looks after Arthur as well as he can, but feels that Arthur needs something to wake him up. Suddenly Arthur begins to take an interest in a boy who is a great naturalist, and in his collection of birds' eggs (the boy's nickname is 'Madman'); Tom thinks that this is just the thing. He invites Madman to supper and they all plan a great birds-nesting expedition together.

ACT III.

Coming home after their expedition they throw stones at a guinea-hen, and are seen by the farmer and chased by the farmer's men. They see a Prefect and go and surrender to him. The Prefect has a great argument with the farmer, who wants half-a-sovereign in compensation, although the guinea-hen was not hurt. In the end, after a thrilling dispute [a lot of agitated recitative here], they agree to pay three shillings, and the Prefect, as they all go back to school, gives them some good advice about keeping out of trouble in future.

Now all that is very brief and bald, is it not? But, of course, there is a lot of detail to be worked in when the libretto (or word-book of the opera) is written, and those who have read *Tom Brown's Schooldays* will see that quite an exciting little opera could be made out of the incidents.

Two Ways of Doing It

Now there are two ways of setting the words:

(a) We can set them so as to make a lot of opportunities for pleasant music.

(b) We can set them so as to make the tale *really* live.

And either of these ways might be quite successful.

The Musical Way

Suppose we try the first way. We shall have, to begin with, a long chorus of boys back from the holidays, saying 'How jolly to be back at School', or words to that effect. Then we shall have a bit of recitative for the Matron as she says that Tom is invited to tea in the Head's drawing-room. And we shall have solos from various boys, telling at great length what they did in the holidays, or what they mean to do at school this term, and there will be various little bits of fun in between the solos, to keep things going. The first scene will then close with a solo from Tom, who is wondering why on earth the Head has invited him to tea, with little bits of chorus by the other boys, saying '*We* wonder too'. This chorus will work up loudly and excitedly as Tom goes off the stage to see the Head and the curtain falls.

And all those solos and choruses will be beautiful tunes, so that as you hear them you will be saying, What lovely music! (for of course *our* music would be lovely, wouldn't it?). But, as you can see, the Scene will not be very much like real life because schoolboys do not make soliloquies and long speeches while their companions stand quietly by. Probably that scene would have about three good set choruses, and about five good solos, and little bits of recitative here and there when we wanted rapid dialogue such as could not well be set to a real 'tune'.

The Dramatic Way

Now imagine the other way of setting. This time we are not going to think so much of the music, though, of course, we shall try to make that as good as possible; we are going to think of making the schoolboys lifelike, so that any old Rugby boy present when our Opera is given will say, 'That's just what *did* happen on the first day of term!' Of course, we shall have singing instead of speaking, but it will not be so much in long tunes as in short natural bits of recitative, only rising to a tune or chorus here or there in some very suitable place.

The Two Ways Compared

If you took the first setting you would find it had in it a lot of pieces that you could sing at a school concert, quite apart from the opera and just as ordinary songs or choruses; if you took the second there would be very little you could take apart in that way, because it would all be just suitable for its special purpose and for no other.

Both these ways of writing an opera may be quite good, but the first will make a more *musical* opera, and the second a more *dramatic* one.

Now the early operas, as you have seen, were dramatic operas, but very soon composers began to make them less dramatic and more musical. They began to put long tunes into the operas, and very beautiful and often difficult ones. When the performance arrived at one of these, the singer who had to give it would go to the front of the stage and sing it more like a concert song than a bit of a play, and meantime the other characters of the play had to stand quietly by and listen. So you see the plot could not move very quickly, for it was always being held up by some long song. Yet, as *music,* many of the operas of this period were very beautiful.

Both in Italy and in France such operas as these were very fashionable, and opera singers who had lovely voices, and who could do justice to the difficult music, earned enormous fees. Opera Houses were opened everywhere. The first one was opened at Venice in 1637, and in that city opera was so popular that even the nuns had performances of it in their convents. Half a century after Opera began it had almost ceased to be dramatic, and was just a pleasant musical entertainment, and half a century later still, so much was thought of good opera singers that they lived almost like kings and queens and made huge fortunes.

Opera in France

A great opera composer in France was Lully, who was under the patronage of Louis XIV. He had been born in Florence, where a monk taught him to sing. A French princess took him home with her as a scullion, and he used to sing and play his fiddle in the kitchen. One of the princess's guests heard him one day and spoke to his mistress about him; she then promoted him, making him a fiddler in her private band. Then he made up a song poking fun at the princess and she found it out and dismissed him, but this turned out well for him, for King Louis (then a youth of fifteen) took him into his famous band of 'Les Vingt-quatre Violons du Roi', and later started a new and additional band, called 'Les Petits Violons', with Lully as the master of it.

Lully became both a clever courtier and a clever composer, and collaborated with the great Molière in writing Ballets for performance at Court, and also wrote operas that were very graceful and pleasant. He was a horrid character, but made a lot of money by pleasing people.

This is just a glimpse at the life of a successful opera composer of the seventeenth century. It will at any rate show you how popular opera had become amongst royal and aristocratic people. Lully had an English pupil called Pelham Humphrey, and Pelham Humphrey was one of the masters of Purcell. And in that way something of Lully's graceful way of writing tunes, and his style of dramatic recitative, crept into English music.

Opera in England

Purcell himself, as you know, wrote a good deal of music for stage plays, and one or two real Operas, and he also set some Ballets, or dance pieces. The earliest opera in the world that is still performed is a very fine one by Purcell—*Dido and Aeneas:* he wrote it for the pupils of a ladies' school near London. After Purcell was dead Handel came to London and for years wrote operas. He wrote them in Italian, which was the

GLUCK

fashionable language for opera, most of the best singers then being Italian. His operas were much more musical than dramatic, and you never hear one of them to-day, though some of the Handel songs you hear at concerts come from his operas.

Gluck (1714-87)

Roughly half a century later than Lully came Gluck, a great reformer of opera. He was a German. He came to England, but his operas could not then compete with those of Handel. After many years his works took on a new style, and then they made him famous. He realized that opera had become too entirely musical, and he started to make it dramatic once more. At first people did not like this, but by and by they saw Gluck's point.

Just to illustrate this, in his famous opera *Orpheus*, which you can still sometimes see (it is the next earliest opera still performed after Purcell's *Dido)*, he made the chorus move about the stage and take part in the play, instead of standing on each side of the stage and just singing. Also he used his orchestra very cleverly. And his Ballets in *Orpheus* were really a part of the play, and, indeed, one of the most important parts, instead of being a bit of entertainment stuck in without much reference to the plot.

Mozart's Operas

Mozart's operas are very beautiful, though some of them have silly stories, for he was one of those men who could set anything to music—and to lovely music, too. You ought to know the names of one or two of the best.

> *Figaro* (*Feeg*-gar-o).
>
> *Don Giovanni* (Don Jo-*vahn*-nee).
>
> *The Magic Flute.*
>
> *The Seraglio* (Say-*rah*-lee-o).

All these can often be heard. You would probably like *The Magic Flute* best.

Some Other Opera Composers

Beethoven only wrote one opera, *Fidelio* (Fee-*day*-lee-o).

Weber(*Vay*-ber), a German, wrote *Der Freischütz*, (something between *Fry*-sheets and *Fry*-shoots; it cannot quite be spelt in English) and *Oberon*.

Rossini (Ross-*een*-ee), an Italian, wrote *The Barber of Seville* and *William Tell*.

Bizet (Bee-*zay*), a Frenchman, wrote *Carmen*.

Gounod (Goo-*no*), a Frenchman, wrote *Faust*.

Some more operas and opera composers will be mentioned later in this book, especially those of Wagner (*Vahg*-ner), a German.

Grand Opera and Light Opera

Some operas have spoken dialogue mixed up with the music. Others are set to music all through, and these last we speak of as 'GRAND OPERA'. An opera with a libretto of a not very serious nature, set to music which is also not serious, we call a 'LIGHT OPERA'. A short light opera is called an 'OPERETTA'. There is an opera popular both in Britain and America just at the time this book is written, called *The Beggar's Opera*. It is nothing but a string of jolly tunes of the time when it was written (two centuries since, 1728), and so is called a BALLAD OPERA.

QUESTIONS

*(To See Whether You Remember
he Chapter and Understand It)*

1. If we were writing an Opera, what two different styles would we have to choose from? Which would *you* choose?

2. When composers began writing Opera, about 1600, which way did *they* choose?

3. And what did the composers who followed them do?

4. What do you know of Lully?

5. What do you know of Purcell?

6. What do you know of Gluck?

7. What do you know of Handel's Operas?

8. Mention any Operas by Mozart.

9. Mention any Operas by Beethoven.

10. Mention any Operas by Weber.

11. Mention any Operas by Bizet.

12. Mention any Operas by Gounod.

13. Give the nationality of Lully, Purcell, Handel, Gluck, Mozart, Beethoven, Weber, Bizet, Gounod, and Wagner.

14. What do you mean by Grand Opera?

CHAPTER VIII

WAGNER

1813-1883

A Schoolboy Playwright

A Leipzig schoolboy of fourteen sat puzzling over something that for days had kept him busy—a grand tragedy he had written. It was based on Shakespeare—characters from *Hamlet* and *King Lear* being introduced, with others too, so that, altogether, there were forty-two characters in the play. And now, at the end of the fourth act, with a fifth needed to finish off the plot, there was nobody left to do it. By one disaster or another all the forty-two had been killed. Happy idea! Let some of them return as ghosts! And so the tragedy was at last finished.

A Mania for Music and Drama

This boy was Richard Wagner and he was always thinking about drama—except when he was thinking about music.

RICHARD WAGNER

Sometimes, sitting at the window, he would see the great opera writer, Weber, pass, and then he would think what a fine thing it must be to be a great composer of operas! And he would sit down at the piano and dash away at the overture to Weber's *Freischütz*, with any sort of fingering so long as he hit the right notes. Then he would take out his own great tragedy and wonder if he knew enough about music to be able to set it as an opera. He got hold of one or two text-books of musical composition at a library, but they did not seem to help him much, and in the end the tragedy never was set to music.

One reason that play-writing and music were so much in the boy's mind was this—his step-father was an actor, and so were one or two other members of the family, so you may be sure that plays and acting were talked about every day in that household.

At school the boy made good progress in Latin and Greek, and he loved Shakespeare and studied him thoroughly. Once there was a competition, the writing of a poem about a school event, and his poem was the best and was printed.

Concert Going

At Leipzig there was plenty of music to be heard. Bach had lived at Leipzig, you remember, and the music at the Thomas Church, where he was musical director, has always been famous. Wagner would hear this sometimes—especially as he attended the Thomas

School, of which Bach had once been 'Cantor'. Then there were some very famous concerts at the hall called the Gewandhaus, and young Wagner used to go to these and especially delighted in Beethoven. In *The First Book of the Great Musicians* I told how Elgar, at a later date, was 'awakened' by the sight of a Beethoven symphony. Hearing Beethoven at these concerts had a great effect on Wagner in something the same way, and soon he knew well almost everything of Beethoven's.

Learning to Compose

Perhaps stirred by the *Freischütz* overture, or perhaps by one of the overtures of Beethoven, young Richard thought he would write an overture himself. He did so, and managed to get it performed at a concert one Christmas Day, but people only laughed at it, because it was so queerly written and had a bang on the drum every four bars from beginning to end.

At last he found a first-rate teacher (one of Bach's successors as 'Cantor' of the Thomas School). He worked hard at his studies, and wrote pieces under his master's direction until he gained a good deal of proficiency. He still went on poring over Beethoven's scores and hearing Beethoven as much as he could, and all his life through Beethoven was one great influence behind his music.

You remember (from the first volume) what Beethoven did. He made music *express more feeling*— made it more dramatic. And this is what appealed so much to Wagner.

All this time he was studying at the University, but he gave a great deal more attention to music than to his studies there.

The Young Conductor

By and by Wagner got a small post as conductor, and then a rather better one. Then he thought he would like to go to Paris, which has always been a city famous for its love of opera. He went first to London, by sailing boat from a North German port. The voyage was a terrible one and lasted three weeks. He thought of the old legend of the Flying Dutchman, who was driven for his sins from sea to sea, always sailing, sailing, sailing, and he resolved to make this legend into an opera.

Starving in Paris

When he got at length to Paris he had many bitter disappointments. He had finished one opera called *Rienzi,* and wanted them to perform it at the great opera house in Paris. But he could not persuade them to do so, and for a bare living he had to work hard at any sort of musical drudgery he could get. Then he retired to a village near Paris, and worked hard at *The Flying Dutchman.* He put into it some of the salt of the air and the sting of the wind, as he had himself found them in the North Sea, and made a very fine thing of it. But he could get nothing of his performed in France, and at last he went back to Germany—this time to Dresden, where, at length, he had the joy of seeing *Rienzi* performed, and the people in delight about it. His *Flying Dutchman* was performed, too, and he was made chief conductor of the opera house there. So now he seemed to have found his feet.

Some More Operas

The next opera he wrote was *Tannhäuser* (*Tann-hoy-zer*). This is a finer opera than *The Flying Dutchman,* and very much finer than *Rienzi,* but the public did not at first like it, for Wagner was beginning to find his own way of doing things, and it was a different way from that of composers before him.

Then he wrote another opera called *Lohengrin.* Both *Tannhäuser* and *Lohengrin* are very popular to-day everywhere, but in those days they were in advance of their times.

Note this—unlike other composers Wagner wrote both the words and the music of his operas. All the time he was getting more and more away from the idea of those days that an opera was a *musical work* (you have seen something about this in the last chapter). His view was that an opera should be a *drama* (a real strong, fine play) *set to music*—music and words being equally important, instead of the music being the chief thing and the words of slight importance. You see then that Wagner had got back to the old idea of Gluck, who in his time went back to the old idea of the Florentines, who first began opera. But, of course, in Gluck's day music could do a good deal more than it could in the Florentines' day, and in Wagner's day it could do still more. So now, the art of music being so greatly developed, and able to express emotions so clearly and strongly, Wagner had a real chance of bringing into existence not mere 'opera', but actual 'Music Drama', and that is the name he before long adopted for his compositions.

Revolution

Troubles broke out in Dresden. The poor people, who were suffering very much, rioted, and the King and Court had to flee. Then the soldiers got the upper hand, and this time it was Wagner who had to flee, for he was accused of making speeches that had incited the revolutionists. He went to Weimar (Vymar), where his friend Liszt was the opera conductor. But this was not safe, and at last he got quietly away, right out of Germany, going first to Paris and then to Switzerland, where for some years he continued to live.

Meantime, at Weimar, the great musician Liszt began to perform his works, and to perform them very beautifully, so that people realized how wonderful they were, and began to see that their composer was a really great man.

Wagner and England

One year Wagner came to England to conduct the season's concerts for the Philharmonic Society in London. He proved successful as a conductor. One thing that astonished people was that often he would conduct a piece without a score, which is pretty common now but was not so then. Beethoven's *Heroic Symphony* he conducted in this way, but, as you have already heard, he had long known Beethoven by heart.

At last the banishment was withdrawn, and Wagner could return to his native Germany.

In later years he came to London again, to conduct concerts of his own music at the Albert Hall. But somehow this time his conducting was unsuccessful, and it was found better to have another conductor, whilst he sat beside him on the platform in an arm-chair facing the audience.

The Mad King

At that time, as you know, Germany consisted of a number of different states, with their own rulers. The kingdom of Bavaria was then ruled by King Ludwig II, who was very much interested in music, but a little mad. Wagner had written and published the libretto of a wonderful series of four music dramas, to be performed on four consecutive days. It was called *The Ring of the Nibelungs* (or for short, just *The Ring*). To produce such elaborate music drama as this would be very costly and difficult, and the ordinary opera houses were very unlikely to undertake to do so. So in his published preface Wagner asked 'Is the monarch to be found who will make performance possible?'

Ludwig was then Crown Prince, and when he read

this he said to himself that as soon as he came to the throne he would show Wagner that one monarch did prize his genius. And hardly a month after his accession he sent his secretary to seek Wagner. The secretary had some trouble about this, for Wagner had got into debt, and to escape arrest was in hiding. At last he was traced and the secretary gave him a photograph of the King and a ruby ring, and said, 'As that stone in the ring glows, so does my ruler's heart burn with longing to see you!'

This reads like a fairy story, doesn't it? But it is true. And when Wagner reached Munich and saw the King, his debts were paid, and a beautiful villa on the shores of a lake was given to him so that he might live and work happily. Wagner was now over fifty.

Bayreuth

Yet *The Ring* was not first performed at Munich, after all. Others of Wagner's works were given there, including *Tristan* and the very jolly comic opera *The Mastersingers of Nuremberg*, but before *The Ring* could be finished and performed trouble had occurred. Wagner was not always wise, and did many things that gave his enemies a handle against him, and at last, though the King still loved him, he had to leave Munich. He determined to settle in the little Bavarian town of Bayreuth (By-royt), build a special theatre and hold festivals there to which people from all over Germany could come. There, in 1876 (when Wagner was sixty-three), *The Ring* was at last given, and people came not only from all parts of Germany, but from Britain, and, indeed, every country in Europe, and from America.

The four dramas that make up The Ring are:—*Rhine Gold, The Valkyries, Siegfried,* and *The Dusk of the Gods.*

Later Wagner wrote *Parsifal,* a sacred music-drama, which was to be performed at Bayreuth and nowhere else, and so it was, until the copyright expired, and then opera managers all over the world were free to perform it.

The Death of Wagner

Six months after the first performance of *Parsifal* Wagner died—at Venice.

What Wagner's Music Dramas Are Like

Here is a recapitulation of a few points about Wagner's Music Dramas—

1. Except for one or two early works, they are founded on national legend.

2. They are very dramatic.

3. Their vocal music is largely a sort of Recitative, which rises into real songs when the occasion is suitable.

4. They are not cut up into a number of quite separate songs and choruses, etc. Each act goes on without break.

5. The orchestral part is largely made up of 'Leading

Motives', as they are called—little bits of music, each attached to some particular thought that keeps recurring in the play, or to some particular character in the plot.

6. A very large orchestra is needed, and the orchestration is very beautiful indeed, and more elaborate than anything written before Wagner's time.

7. Wagner wrote both words and music of his dramas.

8. He considered words, music, stage setting, and acting equally important, and wanted all to have equal attention.

The Three Attempts at Music Drama

Remember the three sets of really *dramatic* attempts at opera:

(a) Those of the Florentines (early seventeenth century);

(b) Those of Gluck (eighteenth century);

(c) Those of Wagner (nineteenth century).

All these composers were aiming not so much at making the music beautiful (though they did that) as at making the play tell its tale vividly by means of music.

Get the dates of Gluck and Wagner in your head (roughly at any rate). Notice that they are practically just a century apart—

Gluck born 1714: Gluck died 1787.

Wagner born 1813: Wagner died 1883.

Perhaps the best plan will be to learn Wagner's dates, and then remember that Gluck's were a century earlier.

QUESTIONS

*(To See Whether You Remember
the Chapter and Understand It)*

1. When and where was Wagner born?

2. Tell what you remember of Wagner's boyhood.

3. And of his later travels to England and France.

4. What was his first bit of real success, and what happened to destroy it?

5. Who was the conductor who first had faith in Wagner and made people realize what a great composer he was? Where did he live?

6. What do you remember about the King who helped Wagner? What happened in the end?

7. What was the name of the place where Wagner set up his great theatre?

8. Give the names of as many of Wagner's Music Dramas as you can recall.

9. What are the special characteristics of Wagner's works?

10. What are the dates of Wagner and (roughly) Gluck?

THINGS TO DO

1. If you can get hold of a book with the stories of the plots of any of Wagner's Music Dramas, read it. If you are learning Musical Appreciation in a class, perhaps your teacher would read one of these stories aloud to you.

2. Get a volume of Wagner's Overtures for Piano (solo or duet) and practise them (if you are a good enough player; they are fairly difficult, as a rule). Or get them as Pianola rolls, if you have a Pianola.

3. There are a very great many Gramophone records of pieces from Wagner's works. Hear all of these that you can, and listen to them often, until you know them well. Find out where each piece comes in the plot of the drama.

CHAPTER IX

VERDI

1813-1901

The Boy and His Spinet

In a little Italian village, called Roncole, in the year 1813, lived two good people who kept a little inn, and sold groceries and tobacco. Their name was Verdi (*Vair*-dee), and they had a little son called Giuseppe ('Jew-seppy' is as near to the pronunciation as we can get in English spelling), who seemed to have a great talent for music. So they contrived to buy an old Spinet (a sort of harpsichord), and of this their little boy was very proud.

I think they gave Giuseppe the Spinet while he was rather too young, for this tale is told about him. He was trying one day to play notes together so as to make good 'chords'. He found one chord he liked very much, but when he tried to find it again he could not do so. He got into a childish rage at this, and taking up a hammer began to smash the Spinet. Fortunately his father came into the room and stopped him before much damage was done. Verdi afterwards made up for his foolish

GIUSEPPE VERDI

treatment of the instrument, for he kept it carefully all his life, and when, about eighty years after, he came to die, this old Spinet was still in his possession.

Verdi must have been a hard worker and his practice must have been very thorough, for the repairer who mended the instrument wrote inside it a description of the repairs he had done, and ended:

'This I do gratis in consideration of the good disposition the boy Giuseppe Verdi shows in learning to play on this instrument, which quite repays me for any trouble. [Signed] STEPHEN CAVALETTI, A.D. 1821.'

So we see that though in a fit of temper Verdi was capable of damaging his spinet, yet he really loved it, and worked hard to master it.

The Wandering Fiddler

There was a wandering fiddler who used to come to the village in those days. No doubt he was in great request when there were weddings or dances, and perhaps on festival days he played on the village green, which lay just before the inn where the little boy lived. We can be quite sure that Verdi liked to listen to the fiddler. You can imagine him standing open-mouthed, and watching his friend as his active bow brought jolly dance-tunes out of the instrument. And the fiddler, on his part, was very much interested in the boy, and I suppose would listen to his playing on the Spinet. Perhaps the man and the boy sometimes played their instruments together.

Now this fiddler, whose name was Bagasset, used to urge Verdi's father to allow him to become a musician by profession, and in other ways encouraged the boy in his studies. And when, long years after, the little boy had become a famous man, he remembered this with gratitude, and finding Bagasset again (now a very old and poor man), he did all he could to help him.

Verdi and the Priest

When Verdi was only seven years old, he used to help in church as an acolyte (that is, a helper for the priest in the smaller duties of the service). But the music he heard used to take his attention too much, and sometimes he forgot his duties. One day, after the part of the service called the Elevation of the Host, the organ music seemed so lovely that he was wrapped up in listening to it, and the priest had to ask him three times for water, and still he did not hear. So the priest knocked him down the altar steps, and he hurt his head so badly on the floor that he had to be carried unconscious into the vestry.

Verdi as Organist

The village organist was soon called in to be Verdi's teacher, but the boy learned so fast that after a year he knew as much as his master, and then the lessons had to stop. Two years after this, the organist left and Verdi took his place, retaining it until he was eighteen years old. He got a small salary, which was very useful to him, and when there were weddings or funerals he made a little more money. One dark night, when he was coming home from his work at the church, he fell into a deep stream and nearly lost his life. Fortunately a country-woman who was passing just then heard his shouts and was able to help him.

Verdi's Great Helper

In the neighbouring town of Busseto lived a well-to-do man named Barezzi, who was a great music-lover, and played several instruments. There was in Busseto a Musical Society, and this used to meet at Barezzi's house. Now, Barezzi took a great fancy to Verdi, and did all he could to help him. He used to invite the boy to his house, allow him to practise on his piano, and introduce him to all the musical people of the place who would be likely to be useful to him. All this was of great value to Verdi.

At this house, too, he met the organist of the Cathedral of Busseto, and this musician now became his teacher.

Verdi Goes to Milan

The people of Busseto had a fund with which to help clever boys to carry on their studies, and Barezzi persuaded them to give Verdi money to go to Milan to study music there. Milan had always been a very great place for music study, and it still is so. It has a great

Conservatory, or School of Music, and also an Opera House which is famous all over the world.

When Verdi got to Milan he applied to be admitted as a student of the Conservatory. He showed some music he had composed, and also played the piano to some of the professors. After waiting a week he went to ask what was the result of the examination, and was told he could not be admitted. This is one of the surprising things in the history of music—that this great Italian music school should have refused, 'on account of lack of talent,' to admit as a pupil the boy who was afterwards to become the greatest Italian musician of his day.

Verdi as Conductor

Verdi was then advised to study privately with a well-known composer called Lavigna, and under him he made great progress.

Musicians need to take every chance of hearing music played and sung, and so it came about that Verdi attended the rehearsals of the Milan Philharmonic Society, which was then studying Haydn's oratorio, *The Creation*. Three conductors took it in turn to direct the practices, but one day none of them turned up, and the secretary, not knowing what to do, asked Verdi if he thought he could manage to accompany. 'You needn't trouble to put in anything but the bass, you know, if you find it difficult,' he said. The singers, who thought they were very important people, were inclined to sneer at such a young and inexperienced director, but, adds Verdi, 'however that may be, we began the rehearsal, and little by little, becoming warmed and excited, I did not confine myself to accompanying, but began to conduct with the right hand, playing with the left alone.'

Afterwards every one congratulated him most warmly on his success, and it ended in his being appointed to conduct the performance of *The Creation.*

Back at Busseto

When the period of study was over, Verdi went back to Busseto. He had been made to promise, before he went to Milan, that he would come back to be organist of the Cathedral at Busseto when the then-organist, his old master, died. But the priests said that as he had been studying opera-music at Milan, instead of church music, they would not have him. Because of this, riots broke out. The Musical Society, which met at Barezzi's house, was very indignant and broke into the cathedral and took away all its own music which it had kept there. Verdi was for three years Conductor of this Society, but at the end of this period he removed to Milan, with the wife he had married—Barezzi's daughter.

Verdi's Great Sorrow

At Milan he was asked to write a comic opera, but just when he was beginning to be busy with this, he fell seriously ill. This caused him to be short of money, so he had trouble in paying his rent. Then one of his children fell ill and died, and a few days after the other died too. Soon after this his wife died. So in three months he had lost his whole family—and all this time he had to be hard at work writing a comic opera!

No wonder that the opera was not a success. The theatre manager, however, had faith in him and was always urging him to write another. At last he persuaded him to do so, and then Verdi began a long series of operas which, as it turned out, made his name famous all the world over.

Verdi's Operas

The Italians are particularly fond of operas. Indeed, as you already know, we may say that opera was *invented* by them. So Verdi, when he showed what skill he had in composing opera music, became one of the most popular men in Italy, and every one there is tremendously proud of him. There is little need to tell more of Verdi's life. It was a long one, and a successful one, and when he died, at the age of eighty-eight, the whole of Italy mourned for him.

Some of Verdi's Operas

Rigoletto.

Il Trovatore (= 'The Troubadour').

La Traviata.

Un Ballo in Maschera (Oon Ballo in *Mask*-ay-rah = 'A Masked Ball').

Macbeth (founded on Shakespeare's play).

Aida (Ah-*ee*-dah; an opera about Egypt, written for the Khedive, and first performed at Cairo).

Otello (founded on Shakespeare's play, 'Othello').

Falstaff (a very jolly opera, founded on Shakespeare).

Amongst other works than operas the most important is a fine *Requiem* (a mass to be sung for the dead) written in memory of the great Italian poet, Manzoni.

QUESTIONS

*(To See Whether You Remember
the Chapter and Understand It)*

1. What do you know of Verdi's childhood, and especially of his musical doings as a child?

2. Mention all the people who are spoken of in the chapter as having helped him (it does not matter about their names, if you remember who they were and what they did).

3. Mention one or two of his great successes, and one or two of his disappointments and sorrows.

4. Give the names of seven or eight of his Operas and one sacred work.

THINGS TO DO

Get all the Gramophone records you can of Verdi's music and listen carefully, until you know the pieces.

CHAPTER X

THE GAME OF 'CAMOUFLAGED TUNES'

In Volume I of *The Book of the Great Musicians* were given a number of 'Camouflaged Tunes', with directions for playing the game. Here are some more. You remember what to do. You get somebody to play these tunes to you on the piano and try to hear the lower one, and to say what it is. Full directions for playing the game of 'Camouflaged Tunes' are given in Volume I.

A Christmas Tune—

A Tune we all know—

A Hymn we sing once a year—

There is something a little curious about the last two bars here; perhaps you will listen carefully and find it out.

Two Carol Parties in the same street—

A solemn Hymn Tune—

Another Hymn—

A favourite Scots song—

A favourite Hymn—

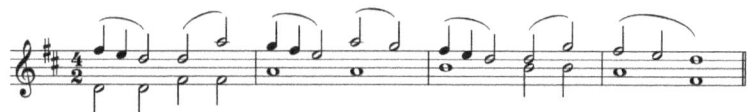

A fine old Psalm Tune—

A soldier's song, with Trumpets above it—

CHAPTER XI

ORGANS

A Human Organ

I do not know whether this game is worth playing. You might try it, and write and tell me.

You pick about a dozen intelligent boys—really serious, well-behaved ones, though, for they must not spoil the game by laughing. (Girls will do if they can whistle.)

You then stand them in a row and make each hold out his right hand (as if for caning, but of course you promise them they shall not have that). You then give each of them a note. No. 1 is to whistle C, calling it *Doh* (and only *Doh*), No. 2 *Ray,* No. 3 *Me,* and so on up the scale, including, I should think, *Fe* and *Ta.*

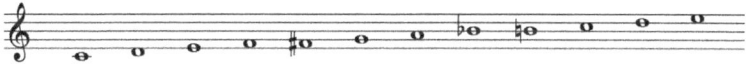

(This needs 12 boys or girls.)

You might make *Fe* and *Ta* (as 'black notes', so to speak), stand a little back from the others, so that you will not forget which they are.

101

THE 'CONSOLE' OF A BIG MODERN ORGAN

The 'Human Organ' is now ready to play, and you walk along pressing down the keys (the hands). As you press each key the boy to whom it belongs whistles his note, and keeps it on until you let his hand come up again.

First of all, for practice, you go up the scale and down again. Then you play a sort of voluntary, like a modulator exercise, bringing in an occasional *Fe* or *Ta*, something like this:

When your Organ can do that sort of thing smartly, you begin to practise tunes—easy ones at first, such as the *Old Hundredth* and *God Save the King*.

Then, if you like, and know how, you can put in a bit of harmony like this:

But you may find that harmony is too difficult for you, and for your Organ, and if so don't trouble about it.

Should you find your organ pipes (for that is what they are) prone to smile, try letting each sing his note (either to its *Doh-Me-Soh* name, or to *laa* or *oo*) instead of whistling it, as it is easy to sing even with a smile on one's face, whereas a quite small smile, by altering the shape of our mouth, prevents us from whistling.

This is perhaps not a game to spend much time upon, but it is worth trying, and your singing teacher may care to try it some time, setting various members of the class to play particular tunes on the Organ, as it is a good 'ear test' to find the right notes.

Tin Whistles and a Pair of Bellows

Now if we wanted to make a simple *real* Organ, how should we go about it? Something like this:

Take a box that does not leak, and a dozen tin whistles. Make a hole in the top of the box for each whistle to stand in. Stick gummed paper over the holes of the whistles so that each will play just the one note you want and no other. Bore another hole in the *side* of the box, this time for the nozzle of the kitchen bellows to go through. Then blow.

Yes! but when the box is filled with air all the whistles sound at *once*, making a horrible noise. That won't do! So next we fix a little cap inside the box under the mouthpiece of each whistle, close it with a spring, and have a string from it running through the bottom of the box by means of a hole we bore for the purpose. This cap is called a 'Pallet'. Now whilst your brother blows the bellows you pull the strings of the notes you wish to sound, and you have a 'Tin Whistle Organ'.

Here is a diagram of it:

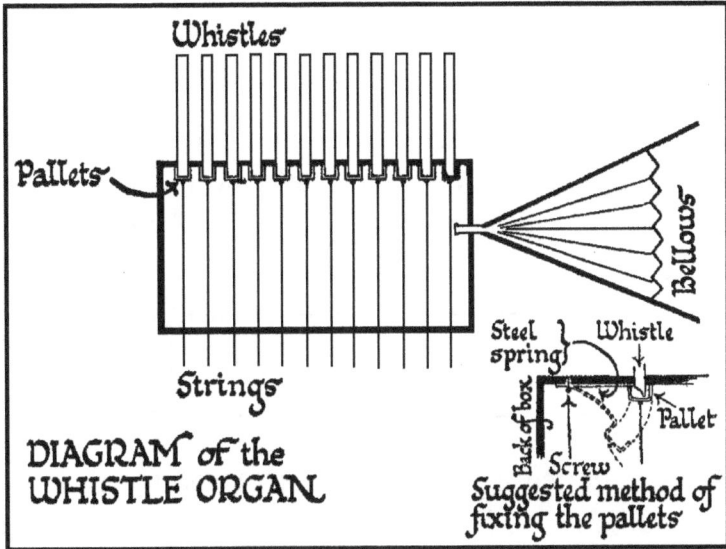

DIAGRAM of the WHISTLE ORGAN

Suggested method of fixing the pallets

I do not say you could actually make a very good Organ of that sort, though a mechanically-inclined boy might, especially if he had an elder brother, or a father, who was an engineer. But I am explaining the subject this way because I think it makes it easier.

Tin Whistles and Toy Trumpets

Next we have a very good idea. We are tired of having all one sort of tone—Tin Whistle tone, so we decide to have also Toy Trumpet tone. We bore another set of holes behind the Tin Whistle holes and (being millionaires) buy a dozen good Toy Trumpets (the expensive sort on which you can play different notes, and we so fix down the trumpet keys that they shall do this), and add them to our Organ. We now have a big cap for each note, so that it will cover the mouth both of its Whistle and its Trumpet. When we pull down the C string, or the D string, we now have both Whistle and Trumpet sounding together.

Yes, but sometimes we may want to play for a time on Trumpet alone or on Whistle alone. So we have another little difficulty to get over. We invent sliders like this:

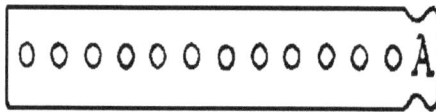

That, you notice, is just a plain strip of wood, with a hole for each note. We have two sliders, one for the Whistle, and the other for the Trumpet. The sliders move under the note-caps (or pallets). The part (A) projects through the side of the box. When we want the Whistle to sound we pull the whole Whistle-slider, so that the holes of the slider come under the mouthpieces of the Whistles, and then, as each pallet is pulled down by its string, the Whistle belonging to it can sound. Or we can push in the whole Whistle-slider and pull out the Trumpet-slider. Or we can pull both out together and then for every note we shall have a combined Whistle-Trumpet sound.

Now if we were to do two things more we should have a small complete organ. *(a)* Instead of pulling down the strings with our fingers we should make a keyboard and tie each string to the back part of its appropriate white or black Key. And *(b)* instead of pulling out the sliders with our hands we should put beside the keyboard two 'Stops' labelled 'Trumpet' and 'Whistle', by which we could do this without leaving the keyboard.

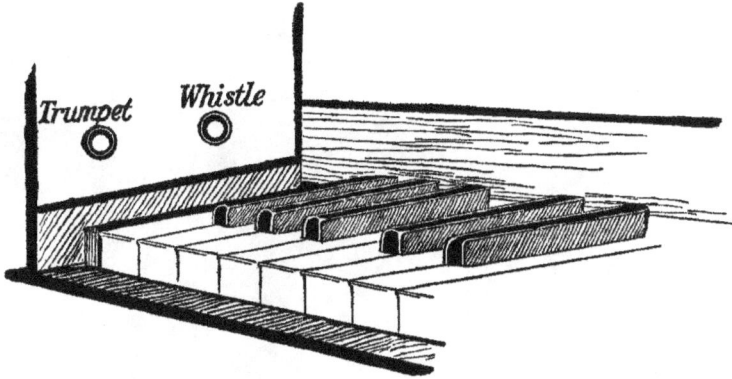

Now for a Real Organ!

If you have read carefully that description you have really got a very good idea of what an organ is like, and you can now go and ask some kind-hearted organist to let you see his instrument. Tell him I sent you, show him this chapter, and say that he is please to take you inside his organ and show you how it is just as I described, except that it has modern improvements, such as:

(*a*) more elaborate bellows, probably blown hydraulically (i.e. by water-pressure) or electrically;

(*b*) far more rows of pipes, and so more stops—say thirty or sixty, and no two sounding just alike in tone;

(*c*) the keys arranged in two or three separate Manuals, or keyboards (so that if the organist wants he can play with one hand on one Manual and the other on another, and can do other clever things); and

INSIDE A BIG ORGAN

another row for the feet ('Pedal Board');

(d) a much neater connexion than our strings between the Keys and the Pallets (perhaps, in a modern pneumatic connexion, or even electrical);

(e) instead of the Tin Whistle stops being all the same length like ours, but having holes in their sides, they are different lengths and have no holes. The big ones play low notes and the small ones high notes. In a very big Cathedral Organ there may be some 'Whistles' (i.e. organ pipes) thirty-two feet long and some but a few inches (every organ, even a small one, has at least one pipe sixteen feet long);

(f) in a very modern organ, instead of the Stop knobs (to pull out), there are little pneumatic pistons (to push in) or some other clever device of that kind.

The Difference between Whistles and Trumpets

You have now got a rough idea of an organ. But before the description is finished you must come back to the Tin Whistle and the Trumpet, and know something about the difference between them. If you break open a Tin Whistle, you find it is just a tube with a mouthpiece. If you break open a Toy Trumpet you find inside it a little strip of brass (called a Reed) which vibrates when you blow the Trumpet, and makes the sound. Mouth Organs and Concertinas have similar reeds (real Trumpets do not, nor do Horns, nor Flutes; but Oboes, Clarinets, and Bassoons do, as you learnt in the Orchestra chapter of the first volume of this book).

Now your organist friend will, tell you that his Organ, like the one I have just imagined our making, is made up of 'Flue Stops' as he calls them (with plain pipes like Whistles) and 'Reed Stops' (with pipes that have reeds inside, like those of a Toy Trumpet). Get him to play you a few notes first on a Flue stop and then on a Reed stop and you will know the difference in a minute, and remember it ever after.

That is all I am going to tell you now about the way an organ is made, but do go and talk to an organist and get him to let you sit by him as he plays. You will find that to play a big Organ is just as fine a thing as to drive an engine or a car.

Some Pictures of Organs

Now, to end with, here are a few pictures of organs, showing how the instrument developed out of something even simpler than our box of whistles.

SCULPTURE OF AN ORGAN OF THE TENTH CENTURY,
AT ARLES IN FRANCE

Note that here we have 'human bellows'—men who blow into tubes, having turns, I suppose, to take breath.

A STILL EARLIER ORGAN

Earlier, yet really more advanced, because it is blown by bellows. The men stand on the bellows to press it down with their weight, then get off till the bellows goes up again, stand on it again, and so on. Some organs on the Continent are still blown in much that way, and the writer of this book used to be organist of a church in Switzerland where this was done.

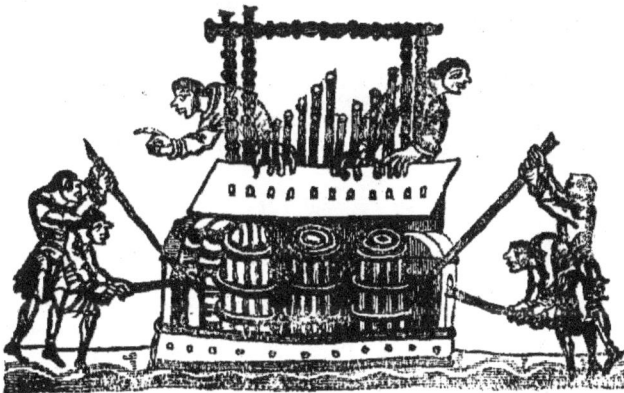

A TENTH-CENTURY ORGAN WITH
FOUR (HARD-WORKING) BLOWERS AND
TWO (BAD-TEMPERED) PLAYERS

Apparently the tenth-century organ had no keys. It looks as though the players stopped and unstopped the holes in the pipes with their fingers.

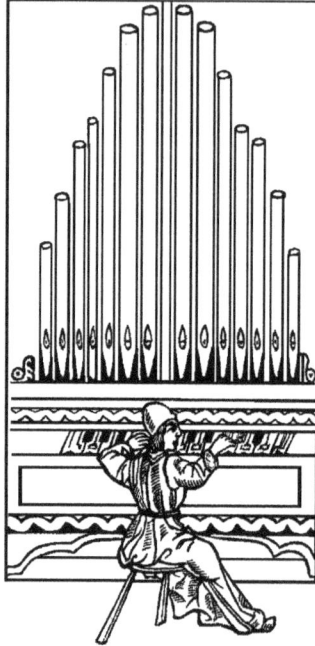

A FIFTEENTH-CENTURY ORGAN, WITH KEYS, BUT THESE SO BROAD THAT THEY WERE PLAYED NOT BY SINGLE FINGERS, BUT BY THE WHOLE HAND.

QUESTIONS

1. What is a Flue Stop?

2. And what is a Reed Stop?

3. What is a Manual?

4. What is a Pedal Board?

5. When the Organist pulls out a Stop what does it do? When he pushes it in, what does it do?

6. When he puts down a key, what does it do? When he lets the key go up, what does it do?

THINGS TO DO

1. Go and talk to an Organist, as I have already advised you.

2. When you come back, write a little essay called 'How an Organ Works' or (if you prefer) '*A Visit to Mr.____'s Organ, and what he showed me*'.

CHAPTER XII

DEBUSSY

1862-1918

ALTHOUGH Debussy died only recently, very little is known about his life—not a twentieth part of what we know about that of Bach, who died in the middle of the eighteenth century. Debussy was a shy man and did not like to talk about himself. What talking about himself he did was done not in words, but through his music—and that, though it tells us a good deal about what manner of man he was, does not tell us what he did in his boyhood, and what people he met, and what difficulties and triumphs he had. So though I have told you, in this volume and the one that went before, quite a lot about the boyhood-life of a great many composers, I cannot do so about Debussy. For this I am sorry, but— there it is!

Debussy at the Conservatoire

This I do know. He showed talent for music quite early, and, as he was a French boy, was sent to study at the Paris Conservatoire of Music when eleven or

CLAUDE DEBUSSY

twelve years old. In the years that followed he won a number of medals for Sight-Singing, a prize for Piano Playing, another for Accompanying, and another for Counterpoint and Fugue. So it looks as though he worked hard.

Now every year at the Conservatoire there is a competition for what is called the 'Prix de Rome'. The competitors are all supposed to have learnt whatever can be taught them about composition, and to need merely the opportunity for quiet practice in composition and self-development. The winner is sent to Rome to a large house called the Villa Medici, where other young musicians and painters are already living. He joins them and works quietly there for two or three years, and is expected to send home every year some composition to show what progress he is making. As you may guess, life in that wonderful city is very stimulating to the imagination of a young genius, and so is the association with other young artists.

When Debussy was twenty-two he won this prize, the composition with which he won it being a Cantata called *The Prodigal Son*. This has been given as an Opera in London in recent years. It is now quite old-fashioned and does not strike one as very wonderful, but it is well written, and it is quite clear that the judges were right in thinking it showed promise, for Debussy's after-career showed that no mistake had been made.

Early Compositions

But the authorities at the Conservatoire did not so much approve of the compositions Debussy sent home from Rome, according to the regulations. The first year he sent a Suite for Orchestra called *Spring,* and the judges said its form was too 'vague'. Next year he sent a cantata for Women's Voices and Orchestra, a setting of our English poet Rossetti's beautiful poem, *The Blessed Damozel,* and the judges said that this was still more 'vague'. Remember this criticism about 'vagueness', for we shall come back to it in a moment.

Debussy in Russia

When his time in Rome was up, Debussy came back to Paris, and then, before long, went off to Russia, earning his living by giving lessons to some young Russians. He took the opportunity of studying Russian music, both folk-music and art-music, and especially that of a composer named Moussorgsky, who was a very free and independent sort of composer—one who went his own way and made up music in the way he liked, and not according to the rules and settled plans of other composers before him. Remember this too, will you? for you will soon find that it has its bearing upon Debussy's own manner of composition.

When Debussy returned to Paris he lived quietly for a time, and then people began to pay attention to him and to perform his music. A choral society gave his *Blessed Damozel,* which had had to wait eight or nine years unheard; a famous string quartet party (the Ysaye Quartet—pronounce Ee-sye, and you will be near it) gave his Quartet; and his Orchestral Prelude, called *The Afternoon of a Faun,* was performed and soon became very popular. This last is the piece of his which we hear most often at orchestral concerts. It gives a wonderful feeling of a sultry summer afternoon, in which we are to suppose a faun (one of the woodland deities—with the face of a man and the legs, feet, and ears of a goat) half asleep and lazily day-dreaming. The music gives us the feelings that we may suppose would pass through his mind. It is a very delicate piece, and, again, vague—like the haze of a hot summer day.

Debussy's Vagueness

That brings me to the point of explaining what I mean by Debussy's 'vagueness', but it is a difficult thing to do. Let me put it this way. He loved in his music to picture nature, but the aspects of nature he loved most were mists and clouds and dusk, and bright sunbeams, and waves in the light of the moon. Now all these things, if you think for a moment, are vague rather than clear-cut and precise, and Debussy's music was often like them. It had its clear lines, but they were so arranged that they gave one the vague feelings of wonder and beauty that such sights as I have mentioned awaken in our minds.

Something about Scales

Go to the piano and play a Whole-tone Scale—that is, a scale with all tones and no semitones, like this:

Debussy had picked up that scale in Russia, where one or two composers had used it a little, and he then used it a great deal more than they did. It, in itself, has a strange effect of vagueness, all the intervals being just alike, so that if you play it up the piano for an octave or two and listen, you will find you can hardly tell where you have got to, whereas with the ordinary major and minor scales the mixture of semitones keeps you alive to where you are, and you can say in a moment (if you have a well-trained ear) 'we have now got to *Soh*', or 'that note is *Lah*'. So when Debussy made a melody out of this scale there came about that feeling of 'vagueness' that I have mentioned.

Something about 'Harmonics'

And his harmony had a vague feeling too.

Go to the piano again, and this time strike a low G.

How many notes did you hear? 'One'! ... Nonsense! you *struck* one note, but *heard* hundreds—and never knew what you were hearing.

Let me tell you something about rainbows. Do you know what colour Homer thought a rainbow was?—Purple! Now Homer lived probably about 3,000 years ago.

But Xenophon, besides the purple, saw in the rainbow red, yellow, and green. Now Xenophon lived, roughly, 2,350 years ago.

But Aristotle saw red, green and blue, and said that sometimes yellow could also be seen. Now Aristotle lived, roughly, 2,300 years ago.

But Ovid saw in the rainbow a 'thousand dazzling colours that the eye cannot distinguish separately.' Now Ovid lived, roughly, 1,950 years ago.

You see how gradually people learnt to see the colours of the rainbow. The latest in date of those I have mentioned is Ovid, who came the nearest to the truth, but even he was bewildered, and could see that many colours were there which he could not, as it were, seize. And some people actually went on, up to six or seven hundred years ago, saying 'a rainbow has three colours.' How slowly people's eyes get trained!

Now apply this to music. If you will listen again to that note G, you will hear not only the note you strike, but also what Ovid would perhaps call 'A thousand dazzling sounds that the ear cannot distinguish separately'. You really hear a *cloud of sound*, something like this:

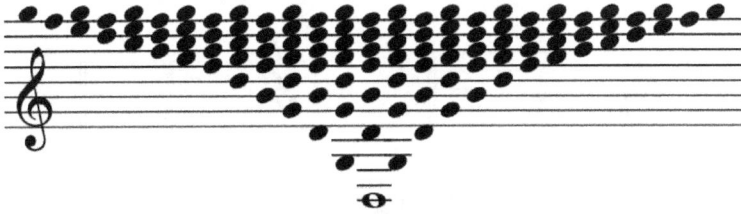

Try the experiment again, this time with the right pedal down, and listen very closely indeed. You can hear that 'cloud', can't you? But I defy you to pick out all the separate sounds given in the diagram, though they are there. Yet if you trained yourself, you could gradually come to recognize many of the sounds—especially the lower ones.

Next time you hear a church bell, go near to it and listen to the 'harmonics', as we call the sounds of this 'cloud'. You will find that you can pick out some of them quite clearly. Debussy was very fond of listening to bells and, with his quick ear, could take in a good deal more, probably, than you or I. At all events the bells taught him harmony—in a sort of way.

Chords

If you look at that diagram again you will find that the first five sets of notes (counting from the bottom) make up an ordinary common chord, and the first seven sets make up the Chord of the Dominant Seventh, which is our most usual 'discord', as we call it. All composers use common chords and chords of the seventh.

Composers have also long used other chords, taking in some of the slightly higher harmonics. But Debussy loved chords made out of the still higher harmonics, chords that he heard the church-bell play when he listened to it very keenly. And if you listen to Debussy's music (his later music, not the earliest, written before he had developed his personal style of writing) you will find a 'vagueness' in the chords that will remind you a little perhaps of the bells from which this composer learnt so much.

How Harmonics Come About

It may be worth while to tell you how those harmonics come about. When you strike the note I told you to strike, the whole string vibrates and makes the low G. But at the same time the two halves of the string vibrate, and give us the two G's an octave higher. And at the same time the three thirds of the string vibrate and give us the three D's—and so on. It sounds a bit unlikely, doesn't it, that a string should vibrate both as a whole and in parts, at the same time? But ask your physics teacher and you will find it is true enough. Possibly your physics teacher can show you some interesting experiments to make the matter clearer.

Debussy's Rhythms

All his life Debussy was not merely a maker of music, but also a *listener.* He heard the bells, and the bugles, and the winds and waves, and other sounds of nature, and learnt something from each, but he also listened keenly to the gipsy bands of Russia, and to the old plainsong in the French churches. The rhythms of the gipsies were very wild, and those of the plain-song very free (I mean, not just two-in-a-bar or three-in-a-bar, but in varying groups so that you could hardly put bars in the music at all). All this taught Debussy something, and in his music you can find the rhythmic influences of the gipsies and of the old church song.

A feature of Debussy's music is that he did not stuff it full of notes, as some composers do. He wrote just as many notes as were needed to get the effect he wanted, and no more. A living Swiss composer, called Bloch, has said that he knew Debussy well and knows Strauss, and has seen both composing, and that when Debussy had written a piece for orchestra he would go through it carefully, taking out every note he could, whilst Strauss would go through just as carefully, adding bits here and there, for the different instruments, until he could add no more without spoiling the piece.

Some of Debussy's Music

Debussy wrote a good deal of piano music, such as *Children's Corner, Gardens in Rain, Reflections in the Water Bells heard through the Leaves, Goldfish.*

Then he wrote a good many beautiful songs.

And for Orchestra he wrote the *Afternoon of a Faun* (already mentioned), *The Sea* (three pieces, one of them depicting morning on the sea, another the waves, another a dialogue between wind and waves), and *Three Nocturnes* (1. Clouds; 2. Fêtes; 3. Sirens).

Then there is some Chamber Music, including the String Quartet.

And there is a very beautiful opera, called *Pelléas and Mélisande.*

Debussy's Death

Debussy died in 1918, when you were __ years old.

QUESTIONS

*(To See Whether You Remember
the Chapter and Understand It)*

1. When was Debussy born?

2. What was his nationality?

3. What do you remember of his early career?

4. What do you understand by the 'vagueness' of his music?

5. What are 'Harmonics'?

6. What is the 'Whole-tone Scale'?

7. Mention all the names you remember of pieces by Debussy.

THINGS TO DO

1. Play any of Debussy's music that is within your capacity.

2. Get some good pianist to play you other pieces.

3. Get *L'Après-midi d'un Faune* ('The Afternoon of a Faun') as a Gramophone record.

4. If you have a Pianola get some records of Debussy's music (there are lots of these).

CHAPTER XIII

MILITARY MUSIC

WE may be sure that as long as men have fought they have had fighting music of some sort. For bold music stirs us and excites us, and makes us feel brave. And for marching it is, of course, a great help, for it not only keeps men in step but also cheers them so much that the way seems only half as long. So we can rely upon it that all the great generals of the past have had music for their armies.

Queen Elizabeth's Soldier-Music

In England soldiers have had their music as far back as history goes. For instance, in Queen Elizabeth's day the soldiers had lots of music. We can see this very quickly if we look at any of Shakespeare's plays, for we shall find that in them all, whenever soldiers are on the march or whenever fighting is going on, there is the roll of drums and the blast of trumpets.

Whatever country Shakespeare's soldiers come from, and whatever age they belong to, he gives them the sort of instruments he himself was accustomed to hear in his and our country in the days of Elizabeth and of James I. There are Drums and Trumpets, of course, as I have already mentioned. But, in addition, there are Cornets (which in Shakespeare's day were wooden instruments, not like our brass Cornets), and Sackbuts (something like our Trombones), and Hautboys (like our Oboes, but rougher in tone).

No doubt Shakespeare had sometimes seen Queen Elizabeth's soldiers marching about the city, and had noticed that these were the instruments they played.

Bands in Charles the Second's Day

Charles II had much the same sort of soldier-music. Like Queen Elizabeth he was very musical, so I should think that he would see that his soldiers had a few good players attached to their regiments, and good instruments for them to play upon. When the King walked out he had a little troop, consisting of a Captain, two Lieutenants, three Sergeants, three Corporals and eighty Privates, with two Drummers and two Hautboy players to provide them with music, and the Queen and the Duke of York had similar troops as their bodyguards.

We do not know what music the Hautboy players and the Drummers played.

Turkish Music in the British Army

It is a curious thing that in the eighteenth century the British Army began to imitate Turkish army music.

Probably this was because the Turks were very fond of instruments of percussion (that is, banging and rattling instruments, such as Drums and Tambourines and Cymbals and Triangles). Such instruments as these, though not very musical, are splendid for keeping time, and helping the soldiers to march in step. And so British soldiers marched to the sound of a few Fifes and Hautboys, with the addition of lots of these noise-making instruments, and they even had one curious Turkish bell instrument which the soldiers called 'Jingling Johnny'.

In those days it was thought to be a great thing to have black men in the band, and sometimes these black men were allowed to behave very strangely, dancing and jumping to the music, or throwing their arms about in time to it. The other day I saw the band of a public school Officers' Training Corps, and the boy with the big drum threw his arms about in a way that has evidently come down as a tradition from those Turkish Band days. To hit the left side of the drum he sometimes used his right arm, swinging it over the top of the drum; and to hit the right side he used his left arm in a similar way. I don't suppose he knew he was imitating our recent enemies, the Turks, but I believe he was.

The Second Life Guards, the Coldstreams, and the Scots Guards had blacks in their bands until about sixty or seventy years ago.

German Bandmasters in the British Army

You know that the British people for some time had a silly idea that they were not musical, and that if they wanted to get good musicians they must send abroad for them.

So during the last century nearly all the Bandmasters for the British Army were brought from Germany, and often the Bandsmen too. If you ask any really old British Soldier he will tell you that in his day his regiment had a German Bandmaster. Indeed, a regiment that had not one would have felt rather ashamed. Occasionally, instead of a German, they would have an Italian.

Nowadays, of course, we have British Bandmasters and British Bandsmen, and there are no better conductors and players in the world. They are most of them trained at the very fine Army Music School, which is called Kneller Hall, near London, and this has become so famous that the Germans have founded one like it. So now they are learning from us, not we from them!

But the French Army Bands are even better than ours in some ways; they have a greater variety of instruments, as a rule.

QUESTIONS

*(To See Whether You Remember
the Chapter and Understand It)*

1. What sort of military music did Shakespeare hear?

2. What other nations have influenced British Army Music, and how?

3. Where are British Army bandmasters trained to-day?

THINGS TO DO

1. Look through any Shakespeare historical play you happen to know, and see if there is any military music in it, and if so, what instruments are mentioned.

2. Write an imaginary description of a visit to London in 1670, and the sight of a procession through the streets with Charles II attended by his bodyguard. Mention some of the great people you happened to see watching the procession, and bring in a little group of the King's choir boys and their remarks on the music (you have learnt something about them in *The First Book of the Great Musicians*).

If you like, put this in the form of a short letter to a musical friend in the country.

CHAPTER XIV

ARMY BANDS OF TODAY

HOW TO KNOW THE INSTRUMENTS

When you hear a military band playing you would, I am sure, like to be able to tell the different instruments one from another. Many of the instruments have already been described in the chapter on the Orchestra in the first volume. But there is no harm in repeating. In fact, it is time you did recapitulate your knowledge of the instruments.

I. — *The Wood Instruments*

1 Flute (or Piccolo = a little, high-pitched Flute).

2 Oboe.

1 E flat (i.e. high-pitched) Clarinet.

8 B flat (i.e. low-pitched) Clarinets.

Bass Clarinet (probably).

1 or 2 Saxophones (probably).

2 Bassoons.

Flute

You all know a Flute when you see it. It is really a simple tube of wood with a hole to blow into and a number of other holes to make the different notes. As you all know, the Flute has a clear smooth sound.

The Piccolo, or little Flute, has a very high tone, and can if it likes play in a shrill piercing way, so as to be heard above all the other instruments.

Oboe

The Oboe is what we call a *Double Reed Instrument.* That is to say, the sound is made by two pieces of thin wood, or cane, placed together, much as you have sometimes placed two pieces of leaf to make a squeaking noise, or two pieces of tin with a piece of tape round them to imitate the Punch and Judy man.

The Oboe has a rather gentle but piercing sound (if that is not a contradiction). It is not smooth in sound like a Flute.

Clarinet

The Clarinet is another Reed Instrument, but it has a *Single Reed*— a single thin piece of wood placed against a sort of mouthpiece.

The Clarinet has a much smoother, fuller tone than

PICCOLO

FLUTE

CLARINET

OBOE

BASSOON, OR FAGOTTO

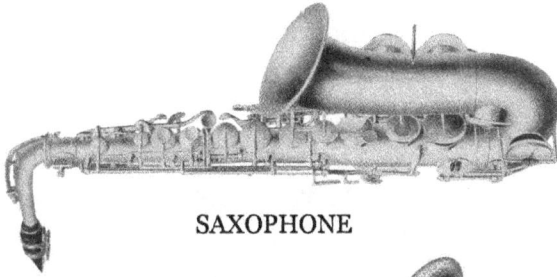

SAXOPHONE

BASS CLARINET

THE WOOD INSTRUMENTS

the Oboe. If you can ever catch the Oboe man playing alone for a few bars, and then do the same with the Clarinet, you will know the tone of their instruments ever after, as it is very different.

You will note that there are in the band more of the Clarinets than of any other instruments. The Clarinets in a Military Band take the place of the Violins in an Orchestra.

Besides the ordinary sized Clarinets (B flat Clarinets), there are in a band one or two smaller ones (E flat Clarinets), and perhaps also one big Bass Clarinet.

Bassoon

The Bassoon is really nothing but a grown-up Oboe, with a *Double Reed* like that instrument. It has a tube so long that it would be inconvenient if it were not doubled on itself in the way the picture shows you.

Saxophone

Though the Saxophone is made of metal we class it with the wood instruments, because it has a reed like a Clarinet. There are two sizes of Saxophone used in Military Bands (just as there are two sizes of Clarinet), a higher one (in E flat), and a lower one (in B flat).

II. — *The Brass Instruments*

3 Trumpets.

3 Cornets.

2 French Horns.

3 Trombones.

4 Tubas.

Trumpets and Cornets

Do you know the difference between a Trumpet and a Cornet when you see them? Look at the pictures of both.

The Trumpet has a much bolder, more bracing tone than the Cornet. But here again, you must watch until you catch the players doing a little bit of a solo, and then you will have a chance of grasping the difference.

French Horns

The Horn is a tube so long that if it were straight it would stick out from the player's mouth for about twelve feet. That would never do, would it? So it has to be curled round and round as you see in the picture.

Horns can play boldly and loudly, almost like Trumpets, or they can play beautifully softly and gently, and then they sound lovely. Just you watch them and listen.

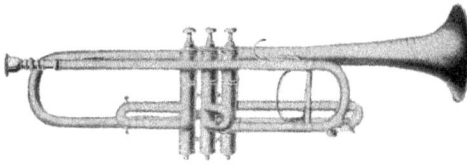

TRUMPET

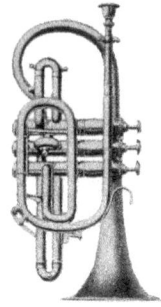

CORNET

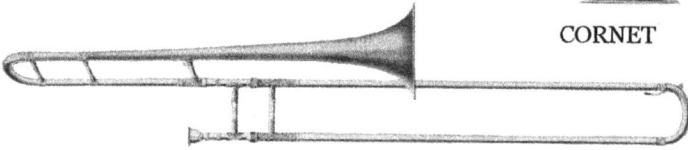

TROMBONE

HORN

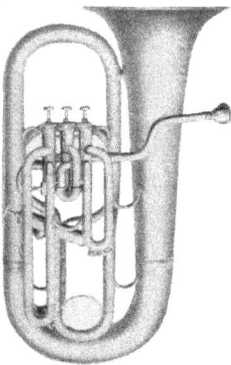

EUPHONIUM

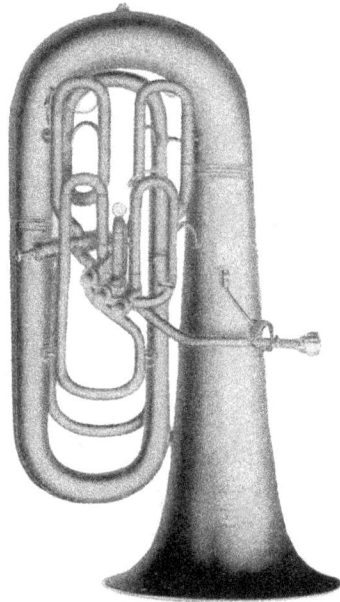

BOMBARDON

THE BRASS

Trombones

I suppose you now know a Trombone when you see it. It is a sort of Trumpet with a sliding dodge for making it longer or shorter, and for so making lower or higher notes.

Tubas

The Tubas are rather like very big Cornets in appearance.

There are three sizes. The smallest of them is called the *Euphonium.*

The bigger Tubas are called *Bombardons.*

III. — The Percussion Instruments

The picture shows you three different kinds of drums:

(*a*) **Kettledrums** or **timpani** (these can be tuned to any particular kind of note, by means of the screws shown).

(*b*) **Big Drum,** which just makes the same low sound all the time.

(*c*) **Small Side Drums** (by a Side Drum we mean one with the parchment at the side—not at the top like the Kettledrum).

BIG DRUM

KETTLE DRUM
(OR TIMPANI)

SMALL SIDE-DRUM

THE PERCUSSION

In addition there are **Cymbals** (brass clangers; you know them, I am sure), and the little tinkling **Triangle** (this also you know). Some Army Bands have more instruments than those I have mentioned, but if you know all these you have got a pretty good understanding of the subject. The proportions of the different instruments vary in different bands.

Whenever you hear an Army Band in future, go and watch it, and listen carefully to the different instruments. Then, when it stops playing, if you can get a chance to talk to the bandsmen, ask them about their instruments, and try to persuade them to play you a few notes on some of them separately, so that you may recognize their tone better.

QUESTIONS

*(To See Whether You Remember
the Chapter and Understand It)*

1. Mention the Wood instruments in a military band.

2. Describe each of them.

3. Of which Wood instruments are there most? Why do you think this is so?

4. Mention the Brass instruments.

5. Describe each of them.

6. Mention the Percussion instruments.

7. Describe each of them.

THINGS TO DO

1. Go and listen to a band and pick out the various instruments.

2. Walk round and round the bandstand, listening to the tone of each instrument.

3. Then stand a little distance away and try to say which instruments are playing—especially when there comes any bit of solo.

4. Get a Military Band record for your Gramophone, and listen to it carefully, trying to pick out the different instruments.

CHAPTER XV

SULLIVAN

1842-1900

THE bandmaster of the Royal Military College at Sandhurst had a boy who could not be kept out of the room when the band was practising. He knew all the bandsmen, and had picked up from them the way of playing many of their various instruments. Indeed by the time he was eight or nine years old, little Arthur Sullivan was quite an authority on the music of a British military band.

And if you go to hear any one of Sullivan's jolly Comic Operas you will very quickly be reminded of what you have just been told, for it will not be long before you will hear some lovely bit of tune creeping in for Clarinet, or Horn, or some other wind instrument. For what the composer learnt as a tiny fellow he went on adding to in later life, and his orchestration is almost always very effective. You can tell as soon as you hear one of his pieces that he loved orchestral instruments, and especially the 'Wind'.

SIR ARTHUR SULLIVAN

Sullivan as Choir-Boy

When he was twelve years old, young Arthur became a choir-boy—one of Queen Victoria's choir-boys at the Chapel Royal, St. James'. If you are a Londoner, or if you sometimes come to London, you can hear the royal choir by attending the Chapel Royal on Sunday morning. You will find that there is a gallery open to the public, and as you look down at the choir you will see that the boys are dressed in a quite brilliant red uniform. Perhaps amongst the boys you are looking at is one of the great composers of the future, for many of our finest British musicians have been trained in the Chapel Royal. Purcell was one of these—only in his day the choir sang in the chapel of Whitehall Palace, which no longer exists.

Arthur and His First Earnings

Sir George Smart was the organist when Sullivan joined the choir. One day the boy showed him an anthem he had written. Sir George told him to copy out parts for the trebles and altos and tenors and basses and he would see if he could get permission to perform the piece at one of the services. In due course this was done, and after the service the Dean sent for Master Sullivan, and told him he was a clever boy, and if he lived long enough and worked hard enough perhaps some day he would write an Oratorio. Then he asked the clergyman who acted as Master of the Choristers whether Sullivan was a good boy, and when the Master said 'Yes,' he shook hands with him and gave him half a sovereign—'which,' said Sullivan, years after, when he was famous, 'was very satisfactory, and the first money I earned by composition.'

Choir Practice

No wonder Mr. Helmore said that Sullivan was a good boy, for he certainly seems to have been conscientious and hardworking. He had a friend in the choir, Arthur Cellier (who also became an opera composer in later life), and these two boys seem to have been trusted to rehearse the others in the music for the services. Sullivan used to conduct and Cellier to play the accompaniments. Mr. Helmore would say on Saturday morning, 'Now, boys, get the music thoroughly well learnt and then you can go as soon as you like. No need for you to stay in during the afternoon.' Then he would leave them, and the practice would begin. But though they wanted their afternoon's holiday, if they did not feel that they had really got the music well into their heads, they came back after their midday dinner, and went at it again, until they felt sure it was perfect.

It seems strange that the boys should have been left so much to train themselves, but, of course, these Chapel Royal boys are a picked lot, and all really musical by nature.

A Good Memory

Once Sullivan was sent to Oxford to sing the solos in an Oratorio that had been composed by the University Professor of Music, Sir Frederick Ouseley. When he came back he was enthusiastic about a certain march he had heard in this Oratorio, and next time he saw his father, he pressed him to get it for his band. But the Oratorio was not published, so Arthur wrote the whole march out for his father, from memory—a pretty clever thing to do!

The Mendelssohn Scholarship

When Sullivan was fourteen he won a scholarship to the Royal Academy of Music. Admirers of Mendelssohn had subscribed to found a great scholarship in his memory, and Sullivan was the first to win it. He studied at the Academy whilst going on with his duties at the Chapel Royal. His piano teacher was Sterndale Bennett, and his composition teacher, Sir John Goss, organist of St. Paul's Cathedral.

Sullivan was always very grateful to those teachers, and especially to Goss, who, he said, taught him how to write effectively for chorus. In any of Sullivan's operas you will find Vocal Quartets and similar pieces which show by their effective style how thoroughly he knew what was wanted to make vocal writing interesting both to singers and hearers.

145

Sullivan in Germany

In those days England was nothing like so musical as at present, and any talented young composer was sent to Germany to study. It was part of the scheme of the Mendelssohn Scholarship that its holder should study abroad, so after a time Sullivan was sent to the Leipzig Conservatorium, or School of Music. Here amongst his fellow pupils was a boy from Norway, called Edward Grieg.

Sullivan worked very hard here, but he said there were too many lessons. The fact is that in music, or anything else, there is a sense in which *nobody can teach us anything.* All the best teacher can do is to show us *how to learn,* and it is our work, and not the teacher's, on which our progress chiefly depends. Well, Sullivan found that there were so many music lessons that there was hardly time for proper practice and home study. His composition lessons were given in an interesting place—in the very room where Bach, when he was the great musician of Leipzig, used to compose his music.

Soon the English boy was popular amongst his fellow students of various nationalities, and they made him President of their Music Committee, and appointed him director of an Opera performance they were preparing. In this way he began to get plenty of experience in conducting.

Best of all, at Leipzig he *heard* lots of music, which in London in those days he could hardly have done, for the London musical public was rather conservative then, and liked to have the same few old pieces over and over again.

Back Again

When Sullivan came back, he at once became well known through his music to Shakespeare's *Tempest*, which was performed at the famous orchestral concerts then held at the Crystal Palace. This made such an impression that it was performed on two consecutive Saturdays. Charles Dickens was there and became a great friend of the young musician, and remained such all his life.

Sullivan as Organist

To earn a living Sullivan became an organist at a London church, and also at Covent Garden Theatre, for sometimes in an Opera a little organ playing is required (perhaps in a church scene), and so there is a regular opera-house organist appointed. This chance of being behind the scenes in an opera house, and picking up all sorts of valuable information about opera performance, was valuable.

Once Dickens and Sullivan went to Paris, and Sullivan called on the popular opera composer, Rossini. Sullivan says: 'One morning when I went to see him, he was trying over a small piece of music as I entered.

"Why, what is that?" I exclaimed. He answered me very seriously: "It's my dog's birthday, and I write a little piece for him every year." '

Sullivan's Compositions

Soon Sullivan became very popular as a composer, and very rich, and the works that made him so were his Comic Operas. Generally the words of these were written by Gilbert, and they were always very witty, and had quite a style of their own. Here are the names of some of them (in order of composition):

Cox and Box.
Trial by Fury.
The Sorcerer.
H.M.S. Pinafore.
The Pirates of Penzance.
Patience.
Iolanthe.
Princess Ida.
The Mikado.
Ruddigore.
The Yeomen of the Guard.
The Gondoliers.

Perhaps you have heard some of these. If not, try to do so. The beauty of them lies in their sparkling tunes, which are just as easy to take in and remember and whistle in the street as the latest comic or sentimental song—but usually far better music.

Of course not all the tunes are equally good, but many are perfect. There has always been a great need of good light music, and Sullivan was the very man to compose it.

Mostly, Sullivan's Operas have spoken dialogue interspersed with music.

Sullivan's Rhythms

When Gilbert had written the words of a new Opera, Sullivan would go through them carefully, and begin to set them, song by song. If you look through a book of the words of any of the Gilbert and Sullivan Operas you will find what a variety of word-rhythms Gilbert used, for he was very clever in this way.

Sullivan's first step in setting one of Gilbert's lyrics was to write down the words and put crotchets and quavers under them, all on the same note but in suitable rhythm, and then do the same thing, in other ways, again and again, until at last he felt he had got the very best rhythm possible. Having reached this point he felt ready to make the melody, and this he proceeded to do—but the rhythm came first.

I think if you really look carefully at any of Sullivan's opera songs you will see that the rhythm is one of the chief charms, and if you then hear it with orchestra you will find that the orchestration is another great charm.

Sullivan's Oratorios and Church Music, etc.

Besides his Comic Operas, Sullivan wrote a number of Oratorios, Anthems, and Hymn Tunes. For my own part (you must decide for *yourself* when you get older) I think Sullivan is best in his light music. Shakespeare could write both wonderful tragedies and first-rate light comedies, but not many writers can work equally well in two different styles, as Shakespeare could.

Amongst Sullivan's compositions were also some orchestral works and a great many songs. These also seem to me far inferior to his Comic Operas, but, here again, you must make your own mind up when you are old enough to do so and have heard enough music of different styles and different composers to have formed a standard of judgement of your own.

But whatever decision you come to I think you will agree with me that Sullivan was very great as a comic opera writer, and that the fact he has written such jolly works as *The Mikado* and *The Gondoliers* is quite enough to justify the fame that came to him, that caused Queen Victoria to make him a knight, and that brought the boy who had been born in a small house in a poor part of London into a position of wealth.

There are such a lot of cheap, silly musical plays performed nowadays that it is very cheering to find that people crowd as much as ever they did to hear performances of the Comic Operas of Gilbert and Sullivan. Often you cannot get a seat at all unless you book very early.

QUESTIONS

*(To See Whether You Remember
the Chapter and Understand It)*

1. *'Sullivan had a splendid chance because he was born and brought up in a musical atmosphere.'* Suppose any one asked you what that meant, what facts about Sullivan's early life would you give them to explain it?

2. Where did Sullivan go to study?—two places, please! Mention one of his teachers and one of his fellow pupils.

3. What is your idea about the statement: 'In music, or anything else, there is a sense in which nobody can teach us anything.' It seems worth discussing!

4. Give the names of as many of Sullivan's Comic Operas as you can remember.

5. Who generally wrote the words of his Comic Operas?

6. What do you remember about the rhythms of the poetry and the music?

THINGS TO DO

1. You can buy a great deal of Sullivan's music in the form of Gramophone records. Try to get some, and listen to and learn as many pieces as possible.

2. Some whole Comic Operas are done as Gramophone records. If you can buy or borrow a set of any Opera, get the book of words and give a performance of the whole piece, reading the dialogue in between the musical pieces. You may have to divide this into two or three performances, an Act at a time.

3. You can get the Comic Operas in a piano arrangement (often not difficult), and you will do your piano sight-reading a lot of good, and pick up a great many jolly tunes, by going through an Opera on the piano.

4. Ask your English Teacher to set as a class subject for composition, Arthur Sullivan and His Comic Operas.

www.ingramcontent.com/pod-product-compliance
Lightning Source LLC
Chambersburg PA
CBHW030012110426
42741CB00032B/393